PRESENTED TO:

_____

FROM:

_____

The Spiritual Warfare
ANSWER BOOK

DAVID JEREMIAH

THOMAS NELSON
Since 1798

The Spiritual Warfare Answer Book

© 2016 by Dr. David Jeremiah

Previously published with the title *Answers to Questions About Spiritual Warfare.*

Published in Nashville, Tennessee, by Thomas Nelson. Thomas Nelson is a registered trademark of HarperCollins Christian Publishing, Inc.

Published in association with Yates & Yates (www.yates2.com).

Thomas Nelson titles may be purchased in bulk for educational, business, fund-raising, or sales promotional use. For information, please e-mail SpecialMarkets@ThomasNelson.com.

Unless otherwise noted, Scripture quotations are taken from the New King James Version®. © 1982 by Thomas Nelson. Used by permission. All rights reserved.

Scripture quotations marked KJV are taken from the King James Version.

Scripture quotations marked NIV are taken from the Holy Bible, New International Version®, NIV®. Copyright © 1973, 1978, 1984, 2011 by Biblica, Inc.® Used by permission of Zondervan. All rights reserved worldwide. www.zondervan.com. The "NIV" and "New International Version" are trademarks registered in the United States Patent and Trademark Office by Biblica, Inc.®

Italics in Scripture indicate the author's emphasis.

ISBN-13: 978-0-7180-9146-0

Printed in China

16 17 18 19 20 LEO 5 4

Contents

GOD'S ARMORY

The Shield of Faith—Ephesians 6:16

The Helmet of Salvation—Ephesians 6:17

The Sword of the Spirit—Ephesians 6:17

God's Armor—Ephesians 6:10–11

The Warfare of Prayer

Conclusion

Introduction

Microeconomics is about your ATM activity; macroeconomics is about global financial markets. There is a big picture and a small picture to everything—even the spiritual life.

Understandably, most people focus on the *micro* issues in life—what's happening to me today. But without a solid biblical backdrop (the *macro* view), today's challenges can be misunderstood and can cause discouragement. The biblical context for viewing all of life's events is called *spiritual warfare*—the age-old conflict between the kingdom of darkness and the kingdom of light. Paul says in Colossians 1:13 that God "has delivered us from the power of darkness and conveyed us into the kingdom of the Son of His love."

The ruler of the powers of darkness, Satan, is none too happy about what God has accomplished in Christ. So Satan's main goal is to destroy the faith of Christians by getting us to doubt God's goodness, love, forgiveness, protection, provision, and promises. When Satan choreographs difficult circumstances in our lives, it is not just to inflict pain; it is for the purpose of destroying our trust in God.

We know from Scripture that Satan will not win the spiritual war, but every time he gets a Christian to give up on God, he wins a spiritual battle. The Bible begins (Genesis 3:1–5) and ends (Revelation 20:8) with Satan attempting to deceive humanity *in order to make God look bad.*

The Spiritual Warfare Answer Book reveals Satan's strategies against God and man—the big picture. But it also describes the Christian's path to spiritual victory: how to defeat Satan and remain faithful to God in life's most challenging moments.

Although Satan has been given temporary freedom to oppose God in this world (1 John 5:19), Christ came to ultimately destroy his efforts (1 John 3:8). In the interim, God gives us promises and power by which we can win every spiritual battle (1 Corinthians 10:13).

Terms of Engagement

Fight the good fight of faith.

1 Timothy 6:12

Why study spiritual warfare?

Biblically and practically speaking, we are in a spiritual war. The Christian's spiritual enemy is not in uniform, and he doesn't meet us on an identifiable battlefield. He uses ruthless and unconventional tactics such as deceit, deflection, and disguise.

A large number of pastors and teachers, however, ignore or downplay spiritual warfare to the point that many professing Christians don't even know they're in a war. This lack of awareness puts Christians in serious danger. The church of Jesus Christ needs to know its enemy and his strategies. Above all, Christians need to know how to gain victory over this enemy.

Two things are happening today that I never thought I would live to see. First, spiritual warfare is getting much more intense as Satan's attacks become bolder. Second, as mentioned above, too many Christians are not taking spiritual warfare seriously or even believing such a war is going on. Taken together, these two factors mean we have a crisis on our hands. When the danger increases and our awareness decreases, someone needs to sound an alarm to prevent disaster.

We are in a SPIRITUAL *war.*

Are we really in a war?

Be assured, spiritual warfare is a reality in the life of every believer. When you open the pages of the New Testament, there is no shortage of passages that characterize the Christian as a warrior and the Christian life as a battle. We are called to a grim struggle with unseen forces, and the fight is real.

> This charge I commit to you, son Timothy, according to the prophecies previously made concerning you, that by them you may wage the good warfare. (1 Timothy 1:18)

> Fight the good fight of faith, lay hold on eternal life. (1 Timothy 6:12)

> I have fought the good fight, I have finished the race, I have kept the faith. (2 Timothy 4:7)

You therefore must endure hardship as a good soldier of Jesus Christ. (2 Timothy 2:3)

No one engaged in warfare entangles himself with the affairs of *this* life, that he may please him who enlisted him as a soldier. (2 Timothy 2:4)

Watch, stand fast in the faith, be brave, be strong. (1 Corinthians 16:13)

Commenting on these passages, pastor and writer J. C. Ryle said this: "Words such as these appear to me clear, plain, and unmistakable. They all teach one and the same great lesson, if we are willing to receive it. That lesson is, that true Christianity is a struggle, a fight, and a warfare."[1]

Don't Believe in a Devil

Men don't believe in a devil now,
    As their fathers used to do;
They've forced the door of the broadest creed
    To let his majesty through;
There isn't a print of his cloven foot,
    Or a fiery dart from his bow,
To be found in earth or air to-day,
    For the world has voted so.

But who is mixing the fatal draft
    That palsies heart and brain,
And loads the earth of each passing year
    With ten hundred thousand slain?
Who blights the bloom of the land to-day
    With the fiery breath of hell,
If the devil isn't and never was?
    Won't somebody rise and tell?

ALFRED J. HOUGH[2]

Know it or not, like it
or not, you and I are in
a war! And we need to
begin living as if we were
in a battle for our lives.
Because, in fact, we are.[3]

Stu Weber

Against whom are we fighting?

Be strong in the Lord and in the power of His might. Put on the whole armor of God, that you may be able to stand against the wiles of the devil. For we do not wrestle against flesh and blood, but against principalities, against powers, against the rulers of the darkness of this age, against spiritual hosts of wickedness in the heavenly places.

EPHESIANS 6:10–12

Every time Paul mentions another class of spiritual beings in his teachings, he reaffirms that we wrestle *against* them. The word *against* appears six times in the three verses above. Think of an oarsman rowing his boat *against* the current. He is trying to make progress in one direction while the current seeks to take him the opposite way. Similarly, we are trying to make progress toward the kingdom of God, and Satan turns the current of the world in the opposite direction, creating resistance with every stroke of the oar.

Satan's war against us is organized and strategic. The word *principalities* (Ephesians 6:12) refers to his head officers, while the word *wiles* (v. 11) refers to his clever plans, crafty deceptions, and cunning methods. Like a military general, Satan plans his attacks and directs his demonic forces.

Note carefully how Paul describes this one against whom we are fighting: "For we do not wrestle against flesh and blood." In other words, our enemies are not people. You may think they are, but they are not. Author John Phillips put it this way:

> We must see beyond people. Satan may use people to persecute us, lie to us, cheat us, hurt us, or even kill us. But our real enemy lurks in the shadows of the unseen world, moving people as pawns on the chessboard of time. As long as we see people as enemies and wrestle against them, we will spend our strength in vain.[4]

Satan is the great destroyer. He wants to destroy your life through adversity and by blocking the work God wants to see manifested in your life. Satan does that by discouraging you, by dissipating your time and energy, and by making a frontal assault on your weak areas that lead you to sin. Satan wants to disrupt your walk with God, ruin your testimony, and destroy your life.

Paul gives the following instruction in Ephesians 6: "My brethren, be strong" (v. 10). Why? So we can enter this battle and fight against the enemy who is against us. This is not a fight only for the apostles. This is not a fight only for pastors. This is not a fight only for deacons or other church leaders. This is a fight for the brethren, for all of us together—the brothers and the sisters in Christ's family. The lines have been drawn. Our enemy, with whom we are involved in mortal combat, is none other than Satan himself. The Lord and the brethren, His people, are battling against Satan and his demons.

How can I be certain I've been called to battle?

You may be wondering, *Maybe I haven't been called to this fight. You know, I'm really not the warrior type.* Well, you may not be acting like a warrior, but if you're a Christian, you're in the army. All believers have been drafted, and either you're going to help fight, or you're going to stand in the background and be miserable.

Again, we hear from J. C. Ryle:

The true Christian is called to be a soldier and must behave as such from the day of his conversion to the day of his death. He is not meant to live a life of religious ease, indolence, and security. He must never imagine for a moment that he can sleep and doze along the way to heaven.[5]

It seems that much of the theology we're exposed to today is about how we can make things better for ourselves: how we can get more money, how we can have more joy, how we can accumulate bigger and better things. Too often, the church's message has become about *us*. But when we study the Bible, we realize that Christianity isn't about making our lives trouble-free. It's about becoming worthy soldiers for Jesus Christ. And that's the spirit of godly soldiers: not looking for the easiest way, but asking for God's help to be prepared for what's ahead.

In order to stand strong against our enemy, we must understand how Satan goes about accomplishing his purposes. I paged through the Bible and wrote down the verbs describing his activity: Satan *beguiles, seduces, opposes, resists, deceives, sows terror, hinders, buffets, tempts, persecutes, blasphemes*—and more. There are no edifying verbs associated with Satan. His goal is to diminish and deface the glory of God. And in pursuit of that goal, Satan is utterly deceitful, divisive, and destructive.

How can I be a courageous warrior for God when I feel powerless?

O nce we understand the fact that we're in a spiritual battle, one of the first thoughts that tends to come to mind is *I am not capable of fighting in this war.* The reality is, this is a tough war. Letting fear or your own inadequacies keep you from the battle is not an option. Every Christian, regardless of age or maturity, is called by God to be fearless. And we do not have to fear, because we are never going to be asked to fight this war in our own strength. God promises to strengthen us with His might.

In the book of Ephesians, the apostle Paul provides a word of encouragement: "Be strong in the Lord and in the power of His might" (Ephesians 6:10). And 2 Timothy 1:7 tells us that "God has not given us a spirit of fear, but of power." These passages remind us that the strength and power for the battle are gifts from the Lord. Isn't that a great encouragement? God Almighty has promised us, His soldiers, that He will protect us and keep us strong. We can therefore go boldly to the front lines, knowing that the Christian is not commanded to be courageous in his own strength but instead to be emboldened by the power of Another—and that Other is Jesus Christ.

More than a century ago, J. C. Ryle wrote:

> The saddest symptom about many so-called Christians is the utter absence of anything like conflict and fight in their Christianity. They eat, they drink, they dress, they work, they amuse themselves, they get money, they spend money, they go through a scanty round of formal religious services once or twice every week. But the great spiritual warfare—its watchings and strugglings, its agonies and anxieties, its battles and contests—of all this they appear to know nothing at all.[6]

The Christian is not commanded to be courageous in his own strength but to be emboldened by the power of *Another*—and that Other is Jesus Christ.

Behind
Enemy Lines

*Be sober, be vigilant; because
your adversary the devil walks
about like a roaring lion, seeking
whom he may devour.*

1 PETER 5:8

Why is it important to understand the enemy?

Before you fight a war, it's always a good thing to know something about your enemy. Nowhere is this statement truer than in the spiritual realm.

Many Christians do not take the enemy seriously because they don't know enough about him to take him seriously. In fact, Satan's cleverest strategy is to make us believe that he does not exist or that he's not a real threat. Some Christians do not even believe in a literal devil. Instead, they believe he is a biblical symbol for evil. But that is not the position of the Bible. The devil is every bit as real as God is. It's hard for a symbol to do the things attributed to Satan in Scripture: deceiving, murdering, tempting, destroying, lying, accusing, and controlling.

In the famous exchange between God and Satan in Job 1, God asked Satan from where he had come. The devil answered, "From going to and fro on the earth, and from walking back and forth on it" (Job 1:7). Satan is active on the earth today, involved in human affairs. In fact, the whole world is under his control (1 John 5:19). God has given Satan authority on the earth for a while, and God will one day take back that control. In the meantime, anyone living on planet Earth is subject to the devil's actions. And we must keep our guard up against him.

In the book *The Art of War,* written twenty-six hundred years ago, author Sun Tzu observed:

> If you know the enemy and know yourself, you need not fear the result of a hundred battles. If you know yourself but not the enemy, for every victory gained you will also suffer a defeat. If you know neither the enemy nor yourself, you will succumb in every battle.[7]

Is it possible for Christians to become preoccupied with the study of Satan and his demons?

There are two extremes we should avoid. If you hold the position that you don't want to know anything about this subject of the enemy and his forces and you aren't going to study it, then you give Satan an advantage through your ignorance of him. On the other hand, if you think you need to know all there is to know about Satan and you read just about every word in print about him, then you will fail to focus on other important truths in Scripture that God wants you to study. Know your enemy, but don't become preoccupied with Satan and his demons.

What do we know about Satan's origin?

Satan's original name was Lucifer, which means "shining one," "morning star," or "son of the morning." And strange as it may sound, he came from heaven. Lucifer was the chief of the cherubim—the highest order of angels. And before the fall, he was in Eden, the garden of God, and he had access to the throne of God (Ezekiel 28:13–14).

We also know that Lucifer was "full of wisdom and perfect in beauty" (Ezekiel 28:12). In fact, Ezekiel 28:13 describes the beauty of Lucifer with gems that reflected the glory of God: "sardius, topaz, and diamond, beryl, onyx, and jasper, sapphire, turquoise, and emerald with gold." No creature had been so fully prepared to reflect the glory of God.

This same passage in Ezekiel also gives us a musical description: "The workmanship of your timbrels and pipes was prepared for you on the day you were created" (v. 13). God had given Satan the very special commission to minister unto Him and cover His glory with music through worship and praise. Of Lucifer's musical abilities, Terry Law has written: "Pipes apparently were built into his very body. . . . He was a master musician."[8] He was a walking orchestra. And that was the distinctive purpose that God gave him: Lucifer was one of God's best works, created to praise God in heaven.

From the pomp and beauty of heaven, this glorious creation will be "brought down to Sheol, to the lowest depths of the Pit" (Isaiah 14:15). All his beauty will be gone. In the epic poem *Paradise Lost* by John Milton, we see this illustrated. There is a battle in heaven as Satan and his followers fight against God for supremacy. After being defeated and chained in a lake of fire, Satan is still not willing to accept defeat. Satan would rather be a king in hell than a servant in heaven. In fact, so great is Satan's arrogance that, even after being cast out of heaven, he has continued to work to subvert the plans of God by corrupting His most prized creation: mankind. Satan also attempts to make evil seem good as he enchants human beings with false gods. From the glories of heaven where he was created, Satan has fallen, and his ultimate destination for all eternity will be a pit.

Satan would rather BE A KING in hell than a servant in heaven.

What caused Lucifer to fall from heaven?

Lucifer was perfect "till iniquity was found in [him]" (Ezekiel 28:15). Isaiah 14:13–14 tells us what happened in Lucifer's heart when he rebelled against God:

> You have said in your heart: "I will ascend into heaven, I will exalt my throne above the stars of God; I will also sit on the mount of the congregation on the farthest sides of the north; I will ascend above the heights of the clouds, I will be like the Most High."

Lucifer's heart was captivated by pride. He decided it was no longer good enough to be an angel created in the beauty of God. Lucifer wanted to be like "the Most High." He desired God's place in heaven—God's position, His power, His perfection, His privilege. And when Lucifer (day star) became Satan (adversary) due to this sin in his heart, he was banished from heaven (Ezekiel 28:16). His proud heart was the reason for his fall, and the Bible tells us he did indeed fall. Here are Jesus' own words: "I saw Satan fall like lightning from heaven" (Luke 10:18).

It was no longer good enough
TO BE AN ANGEL
created in the beauty of God. Lucifer wanted to be like "the Most High."

The essential vice, the utmost evil, is Pride. . . . It was through Pride that the devil became the devil. Pride leads to every other vice. It is the complete anti-God state of mind.[9]

C. S. Lewis

How could a perfect, holy being fall?

Satan wasn't created as the devil. God created Lucifer. Lucifer forfeited that name and became Satan (meaning "adversary" or "enemy") of his own will. But how? Lucifer had no sinful world to lure him, no tempter to push him, and no innate sinful nature to overpower him. How could the first unholy affection arise in an angelic being? The answer lies in the fact that—like you and me— Lucifer was created with freedom to choose.

Each of us has the choice: the opportunity to say yes to God . . . or not. Lucifer chose to use his gift of free choice against the Giver. In his own heart, Lucifer pridefully determined that he would elevate and glorify himself. And that was the first sin ever committed in the universe—the sin of pride.

As a result of his anointed role in the heavens and his great beauty, Lucifer's heart filled with pride, and God cast him out of heaven (Ezekiel 28:17). To this day Satan remains arrogant, prideful, and rebellious against God (Isaiah 14:12–14). It is a warning to us as Christians that, since Satan's personality is characterized by pride, he will tempt us by using the same weakness in ourselves.

It was pride that changed
angels into devils; it is
humility that makes men
as angels.

Augustine

What names are given to Satan in the Bible?

If you read through the Bible and underline the names for Satan, you will discover a great deal about him.

Here are some names of Satan that can be found in the Bible:

- "your adversary" (1 Peter 5:8)
- "the accuser of our brethren" (Revelation 12:10)
- "an angel of light" (2 Corinthians 11:14)
- "the deceiver" (Revelation 12:9)
- "Apollyon," "the destroyer" (Revelation 9:11)
- "the evil one" (John 17:15)
- "a liar" (John 8:44)
- "a murderer" (John 8:44)
- "the prince of the power of the air" (Ephesians 2:2)

- "the ruler of this world" (John 12:31, 14:30, 16:11)
- the "serpent of old" (Genesis 3:4, Revelation 20:2)
- "the tempter" (Matthew 4:3)

There are many names for Satan in the Bible, and all of them reveal him as our enemy.

Does Satan have his own kingdom?

Many theologians believe that when Satan rebelled, one-third of the angels in heaven rebelled with him, came to earth, and now compose his rebel army fighting against God (Revelation 12:4).

Satan is not alone in his evil pursuits: he is the head of his own kingdom (Matthew 12:26). He has hierarchies of principalities, and powers, and angels, and demons; and he rules them all. Three times the Bible calls Satan "the prince of this world" (John 12:31, 14:30, 16:11 NIV). He's also called "the prince of the power of the air" (Ephesians 2:2). As the prince of this world, Satan is in charge of evil men; as the prince of the power of the air, he is in charge of evil spirits. He is spoken of as both a roaring lion and a great dragon and is described as diabolical, deceptive, destructive, rebellious, and filled with hate.

Satan is the second most powerful being in the universe, subject only to God. The Bible says that men are held captive by Satan's power until delivered by the power of the Savior.

Is Satan's army organized?

Scripture clearly teaches that Satan controls and commands a great army of fallen angels. In the force of evil described in Ephesians 6:12, we read that his army is organized and that there is a hierarchy in the domain of Satan:

> We do not wrestle against flesh and blood, but against principalities, against powers, against the rulers of the darkness of this age, against spiritual hosts of wickedness in the heavenly places.

In the Greek language, *principalities* refers to the "first" or the "head officers." The *powers* mentioned here are staff officers, and the *rulers* are divisional commanders. And with this rank and file is the spiritual host of wickedness under the command of these officers. Clearly, there is an organized effort on the part of Satan to do his work in the world. He has arranged his forces against God's people, and we are the target of his schemes.

> The great trouble with the world today and with the church unfortunately, is that they know so little about the devil and his "principalities and powers."[10]
>
> D. MARTYN LLOYD-JONES

Is Satan a god?

The Bible says, strange as it may be, that Satan is a god—with a lowercase "g." Second Corinthians 4:4 refers to "the god of this age." Who is that god? It is Satan.

Satan is the founder and president of his own religion. He has his own church:

> I know your works, tribulation, and poverty (but you are rich); and I know the blasphemy of those who say they are Jews and are not, but are a synagogue of Satan.... Indeed I will make those of the synagogue of Satan, who say they are Jews and are not, but lie—indeed I will make them come and worship before your feet, and to know that I have loved you (Revelation 2:9, 3:9).

He has his own gospel: "If we, or an angel from heaven, preach any other gospel to you than what we have preached to you, let him be accursed" (Galatians 1:8).

He has his own ministers: "Therefore it is no great thing if his ministers also transform themselves into ministers of righteousness, whose end will be according to their works" (2 Corinthians 11:15).

He has his own doctrine: "Now the Spirit expressly says that in latter times some will depart from the faith, giving heed to deceiving spirits and doctrines of demons" (1 Timothy 4:1).

And he has his own communion table and his own cup: "The things which the Gentiles sacrifice they sacrifice to demons and not to God, and I do not want you to have fellowship with demons. You cannot drink the cup of the Lord and the cup of demons; you cannot partake of the Lord's table and of the table of demons" (1 Corinthians 10:20–21).

Satan is the god of this age.

How powerful is Satan?

In 2 Thessalonians 2:9, we read that "the coming of the lawless one is according to the working of Satan, with all power, signs and lying wonders," so we know he has supernatural power. First Peter 5:8 describes Satan as "a roaring lion, seeking whom he may devour." He is deceptive. He is seductive. He is destructive. And Satan is filled with hatred. He has his own armor. He has his own strongholds. He has his own strong men. And he is the power behind the world system.

First John 5:19 says: "The whole world lies under the sway of the wicked one." So Satan definitely has power—power that, were it not for our relationship with Christ, we should fear. But as Christians, we can stand firm on the battlefield because greater is He who lives in us than Satan who lives in the world (1 John 4:4).

The Bible tells us that God has Satan on a

leash (Job 1–2). Our enemy may have a little power in this day—power that has been granted to him under the sovereignty of God—but one day he will be confined forever in the lake of fire with his angels.

Christians have the ultimate victory over sin and death through Christ. Satan's power is power under control—God's control.

Is Satan God's opposite?

We must never underestimate Satan's power, but we also cannot err in believing that Satan is as powerful as Almighty God. Satan is not and never will be all-knowing or all-powerful. He is not the opposite of God.

How did Satan get here in the first place? He is God's creation. So don't be tempted to think, *God's over here, and He's all-powerful for good; and Satan's over there, and he's all-powerful for evil.* That's not true. Satan is no match for God. God has no equal.

How does Satan attempt to deceive the world?

Spiritual deception may be Satan's most insidious weapon in his guerrilla warfare against us. Jesus and the apostles speak of it nearly thirty times in the New Testament. John 8:44 records Jesus' reply to a group of Jews who were resisting His message. Jesus boldly told them that they were children of their father the devil and that they were not hearing the truth because their father's native language was lies. A person's native language is what he or she converses in most easily. And Satan speaks the language of deception quite fluently.

In fact, Revelation 12:9 refers to Satan as the one "who deceives the whole world," and he does so by imitating the work of God through counterfeit and camouflage. Satan's last and greatest deception will be to bring the Antichrist to the world at the end of the age. Initially the Antichrist will be a peacemaker who uses persuasive speech and manifests supernatural powers much as Jesus Himself did. But once people fall for this counterfeit, the Antichrist will lead them not to God but away from Him.

Pastor and theologian R. Kent Hughes explains one of the reasons for Satan's effectiveness as a deceiver and manipulator:

> I am no genius at mathematics, but even with my limited capabilities I could be terrific at math if I worked at it for 100 years (maybe!). If I labored hard at it for 1,000 years and read all the learned theories, I would be a Newton or an Einstein. Or what if I had 10,000 years? Given that time, any of us could become the world's greatest philosopher or psychologist or theologian or linguist. . . . Satan has had multiple millennia to study and master the human disciplines, and when it comes to human subversion, he is the ultimate manipulator.[11]

The devil's disguises are very clever, and he hides in the most unbelievable places. One of his favorite hideouts is religion. He also hides behind intellectualism. He hides in poetry and art and oftentimes in music. He hides in psychology and human understanding. Satan can even use the subtle method of Scripture taken out of context to deceive. When people take verses out of context and use them to prove something they were not intended to prove, those people are falling right into Satan's trap.

Satan never tempts us to believe blatant error: that would be too easily discerned. Satan is subtle, and that is why we as the people of God must stay alert.

How does Satan attempt to imitate God?

Most people don't realize that part of Satan's deception is his skill as a counterfeiter and mimic. Satan himself said, "I will be like the Most High" (Isaiah 14:14). And when you watch Satan at work in the world, it becomes evident that everything the Lord has done, Satan pitifully attempts to duplicate.

Jesus is the "Prince of Peace" (Isaiah 9:6); Satan is "the prince of this world" (John 12:31, 14:30, 16:11 NIV).

Jesus is "the light of the world" (John 9:5); Satan is transformed into "an angel of light" (2 Corinthians 11:14).

Jesus Christ is "the LORD my God" (Zechariah 14:5); Satan is "the god of this age" (2 Corinthians 4:4).

Jesus is "the Lion of the tribe of Judah"

(Revelation 5:5); Satan is "a roaring lion, seeking whom he may devour" (1 Peter 5:8).

Satan attempts to imitate God because he wants to be like God.

How does Satan stir up division in the body of Christ?

I have heard many stories of churches where discord among the members led to an unpleasant split—a division that destroyed the peace and unity in the body of Christ. Let me tell you who's behind all of that: Satan himself.

Satan likes to use the time-honored strategy of divide and conquer. When he was cast out of heaven, he took a third of the angels with him. He divided the first human family, pitting Cain against Abel. He tempted Ananias and Sapphira to divide their loyalty between God and money. And today Satan follows that same strategy. Our enemy continues to bring division to friendships, fellowships, small groups, churches, and church staff.

How? He injects the poisons of suspicion and intolerance and hatred and jealousy and criticism—poisons that seek an outlet in the body of Christ. Oftentimes that outlet is the human tongue: our words. James says the tongue "is set on fire by hell. . . . It is an unruly evil, full of deadly poison" (James 3:6, 8). When we find hurtful words creating division in the church, guess who is delighted?

Wherever you find division, you know Satan is at work.

Descriptions of Satan in the Bible

He is a **serpent** trying to deceive God's people.
- Genesis 3:1
- Revelation 12:9

He is a **bird** trying to despoil God's harvest.
- Matthew 13:4, 19

He is a **wolf** trying to defeat God's flock.
- John 10:12
- Matthew 10:16

He is a **lion** trying to devour God's children.
- 1 Peter 5:8

He is a **dragon** trying to destroy God's Son.
- Revelation 12:1-9

How does Satan use the strategy of destruction?

In Revelation 9:11, the apostle John called Satan "Apollyon," which in Greek means "destroyer." That name really suits the devil, doesn't it?

Satan will do anything to destroy, delay, demolish, or dismantle God's work. Job, in the Old Testament, is a prime example. When God granted Satan access to Job, Satan destroyed everything except Job and his wife. Satan even destroyed Job's health and his wife's attitude toward her husband. Job resisted and remained faithful to God in spite of Satan's testing. At the end of his test, God richly blessed Job for victoriously enduring his trial of faith.

Satan knows he can't destroy God, so his next tactic is to destroy the people of God—to cause adversity in our lives. And he will take any opportunity, however small and seemingly insignificant, to attempt to destroy a lifetime of faithfulness to God. So stay on guard!

Satan knows HE CAN'T DESTROY GOD, *so his next tactic is to destroy the people of God.*

How does Satan use the strategy of distraction?

The idea of staging an intervention in a person's life to arrest the progress of some kind of injurious or unwise behavior is well known. The goal is to break the normal cycle of behavior and substitute clinical help or other better behaviors. Satan, however, loves to intervene in our lives to do just the opposite: he wants to distract us from our healthy spiritual behaviors and tempt us with bad behaviors.

If Satan can distract us from the spiritually productive priorities in our life and occupy us with the things of this world, his intervention will be successful. If we are too busy to pray, study the Bible, serve others, and attend church or Bible studies, then we will not grow spiritually. We will remain babes in Christ.

Of course, there's nothing wrong with being busy—as long as we are busy with the right things and we don't get so busy that we begin to think of our busyness as a way of impressing God. Even that is a trap that Satan uses to distract us from true spirituality.

What are the "wiles of the devil"?

The Bible teaches us that Satan is attacking the lives and the causes that would defeat his plans. That is why all of us who are Christians feel the effects of Satan's presence. He is not after those who belong to him. Satan concentrates his efforts on those who want to defeat him. That's Satan's purpose: to weaken the influence of men and women who know Jesus Christ. And the Bible says Satan has a method for doing this. We are doing battle against "the wiles of the devil" (Ephesians 6:11).

Now, *wiles* is not a word we use a lot in our culture today. To employ *wiles* is to use cunning and stratagems to persuade someone to do what one wants. And I personally believe that Satan has a strategy for every one of us. He knows our weaknesses, he knows our strengths, and he will stop at nothing if he thinks he can victimize us for his own purposes.

The Greek word *methodeia* is translated as "wiles" or "wile" in the King James Version and is the source of our English word *method*. This word is another indication that the one who is planning to attack us is organized and systematic. His plans are the "wiles of the devil" we must guard against.

When we run from the enemy, we open ourselves up to ultimate spiritual defeat.

What are some ways we give ground to the enemy?

When we know what is right and we compromise that conviction in order to indulge in something we want to do, we give ground to the enemy.

When we hear the voice of God speaking to us clearly and, for reasons of our comfort or perhaps even out of fear, we postpone our obedience, we open up the door for the enemy to attack.

The Bible says that the devil, "like a roaring lion," goes about "seeking whom he may devour" (1 Peter 5:8). He wants to so change who we are that we no longer have any power of commitment or testimony. Satan wants us to fall into fleshly things that destroy our ability to stand for the Lord. That's what he seeks to do. Satan wants, primarily, to devour our influence for Christ. And when we run from the enemy, we open ourselves up to ultimate spiritual defeat.

Don't give Satan an opportunity to come alongside and destroy you. Don't turn away from him. Rather, keep him in view and stand strong in the midst of his attempts to destroy.

Are demons real?

While there are some people today who deny the reality of demons, the Bible gives abundant evidence for their existence. Demons are mentioned more than eighty times in the New Testament; and in most cases, we see the Lord Jesus Christ confronting them. Christ knew the reality of demons, and He demonstrated His power over them often:

- "At evening, when the sun had set, they brought to [Jesus] all who were sick and those who were demon-possessed" (Mark 1:32).
- "[Jesus] was preaching in their synagogues throughout all Galilee, and casting out demons" (Mark 1:39).
- "Then His fame went throughout all Syria; and they brought to Him all sick people who were afflicted with various diseases

and torments, and those who were demon-possessed, epileptics, and paralytics; and He healed them" (Matthew 4:24).

- "That very hour [Jesus] cured many of infirmities, afflictions, and evil spirits; and to many blind He gave sight" (Luke 7:21).

Satan does not work alone in his spiritual attacks.

Jesus spoke of the eternal fire prepared "for the devil *and his angels*" (Matthew 25:41). Satan "*and his angels*" are referred to together in Revelation 12:9. In Matthew 12:24 Satan is called "Beelzebub, the ruler *of the demons.*"

These spirits are rational beings, not diseases or ailments or tricks of the imagination. They possess all the attributes of personality. They even believe in God, as James told us: "You believe that there is one God. Good! Even *the demons believe* that—and shudder" (James 2:19 NIV).

Demons think and believe and hear and speak against God's people. They are real!

What are demons?

Demons are Satan's servants, and they are committed to his scheme to thwart the plan of God. Often in Scripture, demons are also called "evil spirits" or "unclean spirits." They are ruled by Satan himself, and they share in his dirty work.

But lock onto the fact that nothing demons do can be outside God's good purpose and design. Never forget this: "Neither angels *nor demons . . . nor any powers* . . . nor anything else in all creation, will be able to separate us from the love of God that is in Christ Jesus our Lord" (Romans 8:38–39 NIV).

Commenting on this truth, John Calvin described God as "turning the unclean spirits hither and thither at his pleasure." The demons are always "warring against [God's people], assailing them with wiles, urging them with solicitations, pressing close upon them, disturbing, alarming, and occasionally wounding, but *never conquering or oppressing them.*"[12]

Just as Satan and the demons share a common origin, a common passion, and a common work, so they also must face a common fate. Paul assured us that Jesus "must reign until he has put *all his enemies* under his feet" (1 Corinthians 15:25 NIV). These enemies include the devil and every demon.

Are there different kinds of demons?

When we study the Bible, we learn about two kinds of demons. They are what we might call "the fallen and the free" and "the fallen and the imprisoned."

"The fallen and the free" are those demons who are creating all the havoc and stress in the world today under Satan's control. Then there are "the fallen and the imprisoned"—a class of demons already imprisoned in a place called Tartarus, one of the compartments of hell. Jude 1:6 says, "The angels who did not keep their proper domain, but left their own abode, [the Lord] has reserved in everlasting chains under darkness for the judgment of the great day." And they will be there forever and ever. They will never get out. And Scripture says it's because they "did not keep their proper domain."

In Genesis we read that when the fallen angels saw the daughters of men, they were filled with lust and cohabited with them, bearing offspring that were half angelic and half human—a superhuman product called, in biblical language, the *nephilim,* meaning "giants" (Genesis 6:1–2, 4). This violation of God-given boundaries so grieved God that He decided immediately to send a flood to destroy the whole earth, keeping only eight souls alive on the ark. And it was because of that sin, when the angels left their proper domain and entered into the realm of human flesh, that those fallen angels were cast down to hell "into chains of darkness, to be reserved for judgment" (2 Peter 2:4).

In every encounter between Jesus and demons in the Gospels, Jesus was the Overcomer. His followers share in that power. When Christ's disciples returned "with joy" from a ministry trip, they reported to Jesus, "Lord, even *the demons submit to us* in your name" (Luke 10:17 NIV). And Jesus answered, "*I saw Satan fall* like lightning from heaven" (Luke 10:18 NIV).

Jude says that God has kept the fallen angels

"in darkness, *bound with everlasting chains* for judgment on the great Day" (Jude 1:6 NIV).

Meanwhile, until that great day, we wrestle and "*struggle* . . . against the powers of this dark world and against the spiritual forces of evil in the heavenly realms" (Ephesians 6:12 NIV).

In this struggle there is Someone who shows us how to endure and how to win, Someone who knew more spiritual warfare than anyone who ever walked the earth. That Someone is Jesus.

Can a believer be possessed by a demon?

Demons are active in the world today, but I believe the Bible is clear that Christians cannot be demon-possessed. First Corinthians 6:19 says, "Do you not know that your body is the temple of the Holy Spirit who is in you, whom you have from God, and you are not your own?" Believers are permanently indwelt by the Spirit of God.

Then, in 1 John 4:4 we read, "You are of God, little children, and have overcome them, because He who is in you is greater than he who is in the world." He who is in us is the Holy Spirit, and he who is in the world is Satan with his demons. And the conclusion is quite clear: a demon is not able to enter and take control of a believer because the Holy Spirit is stronger than any demonic being, including Satan himself. It's that simple.

Christians are troubled by the devil, tempted by the devil, and perhaps even obsessed with the devil, but they are never possessed by him.

A demon is not able to enter and take control of a believer because the

HOLY SPIRIT

is stronger than any demonic being, including Satan himself.

What will ultimately happen to Satan and his army of fallen angels?

The devil and his demons are doomed to everlasting punishment. There is no hope for them because Jesus Christ did not shed His blood on Calvary to redeem fallen angels. They fell from living in the presence of God Almighty as His chosen cherubs of worship. Acting on their own volition, these angels rebelled against God.

One day Satan will be cast into the bottomless pit for one thousand years, and then he and his angels will be thrown into the lake of fire (Revelation 20:1–3, 10). God has already won the victory over Satan and his army. Their judgment is sure: "[The risen Christ] will also say to those on the left hand, 'Depart from Me, you cursed, into the everlasting fire prepared for the devil and his angels'" (Matthew 25:41). We await the day when the sentence will be carried out in complete detail.

God's Armory

Stand therefore, having girded your
waist with truth, having put on the
breastplate of righteousness, and having
shod your feet with the preparation of
the gospel of peace; above all, taking
the shield of faith with which you
will be able to quench all the fiery
darts of the wicked one. And take the
helmet of salvation, and the sword of
the Spirit, which is the word of God.

EPHESIANS 6:14–17

What armor has God given me for warfare?

This war against Satan is not one that we have to go into unprotected. The apostle Paul identified six pieces of spiritual armor in Ephesians 6:14–17, each one dealing with a specific area of our lives.

1. The Girdle of Truth
2. The Breastplate of Righteousness
3. The Shoes of the Gospel of Peace
4. The Shield of Faith
5. The Helmet of Salvation
6. The Sword of the Spirit

Don't be a casualty of spiritual warfare. Get in the battle and stand strong against the enemy by wearing the full armor of God every day!

The Girdle
of Truth

*Stand therefore, having girded
your waist with truth.*

EPHESIANS 6:14

What protection does the girdle of truth provide?

Paul first told us to be girded about with truth, referring to the belt that harnessed a soldier's weapons to his body. Today's soldiers are outfitted with a combat harness, a modern version of the Roman soldier's belt that serves the same function. It allows them to carry all their needed equipment in a confined space under combat conditions. This harness includes pouches for extra ammo, grenades, a canteen, a radio or satellite phone, and other items such as medical supplies or personal articles.

For the Christian, this combat harness is *truth*. Paul says, "Stand therefore, having girded your waist with truth." This particular combat harness is important because of the nature of our enemy: Satan is determined to hinder God's work in our lives. Satan is here to steal, to kill, and to destroy. He's "like a roaring lion, seeking [someone] to destroy" (1 Peter 5:8). He is a liar from the beginning, a deceiver, a serpent. He is the accuser of the brethren. Whatever he says to us is a distortion.

In *The Last Lion,* biographer and historian William Manchester wrote that Winston Churchill "adopted, as a working thesis, the assumption that any given foreign policy statement by Hitler was the exact opposite of truth."[13] It was an assumption that served Churchill well, for Hitler was a liar and a deceiver from the beginning.

We can make the same assumption about the devil. John 8 says that Satan is a liar and that there is no truth in him. Satan comes at us with deception, sham, trickery, and falsity. He wants to entangle us. Notice, for instance, how he has blurred the values of right and wrong in our society. Notice how his propaganda machine—today's entertainment media—glorifies immorality and ridicules biblical values.

That means that Christians must be children of truth. We have to implement truth in our lives. Jesus says, "I am the . . . truth" (John 14:6). John 1:14 says that He is "full of grace and truth." Jesus says that God's Word is truth (John 17:17). He told His disciples, "If you abide in My Word, you are My disciples indeed. And you shall know the truth, and the truth shall make you free" (John 8:31–32).

How do I arm myself with the girdle of truth?

In order to be armed with the truth, we must know the truth—the whole counsel of God. God has put everything He wants us to know between the covers of the Bible—everything He wants us to know about Himself, about His Son, about eternity, and about life. And when we study God's Word, when we carefully learn and then apply its truth, we end up with power in our lives.

Now, you might never memorize the whole Bible, but make it a priority to know your Bible well enough to know where you are going to find specific answers in Scripture. The more truth you know, the better equipped you are to go into battle and be victorious. When you take God's truth and apply it to yourself, then you can embody that truth in your life, and God will enable you to be victorious on the battlefield.

How can I discern Satan's lies from God's truth?

Someone once told me that if you want to identify a crooked stick, the best thing you can do is lay a straight stick down next to it. That same principle works when you're dealing with the deceit of Satan. If you will lay the straight stick of God's Word next to what it is you are trying to discern, you will usually be able to identify Satan's deceitful propaganda.

But I recently read an article written by Roger Olson in which he recommends an additional tool. He wrote:

> I believe it is important and valuable for Christians to know not only theological correctness (orthodoxy) but also the ideas of those judged as heretics within the church's story. One reason is that it is almost impossible

to appreciate the meaning of orthodoxy without understanding the heresies that forced its development.[14]

The apostle Paul warned that Satan takes advantage of us when we are ignorant of his strategies (2 Corinthians 2:11).

What does it mean to live a life of truthfulness?

Truth is objective: either something is true or it's not true. Truthfulness, then, is whether or not the truth we know about God has caused us to be people who are truthful.

If we want to be warriors in the battle against Satan, we must be people of integrity and sincerity. Third John 4 says, "I have no greater joy than to hear that my children walk in truth." In other words, these believers don't just know the truth; they are living a life of truthfulness, a life that is impacted by the head and heart knowledge of God's immutable truth.

Such a lifestyle implies that we are dealing with the realities of sin and our sinful selves. We are not allowing hypocrisy or any excuse to keep us from living the way God calls us to live; we are not condoning sin with either our words or our silence, our action or our inaction. We are seeking to be honest before the Lord and before others; we are not faking the Christian life and putting a spin on what it means to be a Christian. That's what the girdle of truth is all about. It's knowing the truth and then allowing that truth to change who we are from the inside out. After all, how can we have any influence in the lives of others about the truth if we're not living the truth in our own life?

Search me, O God, and know my heart; try me, and know my anxieties; and see if there is any wicked way in me, and lead me in the way everlasting.

PSALM 139:23–24

What is the importance of a clear conscience?

It is not uncommon to hear someone being instructed to "let their conscience be their guide." But this is not always good advice. It is possible to follow one's conscience and do the wrong thing.

Six times in his pastoral epistles, Paul mentions the conscience. He writes about a good conscience and a pure conscience, but he also says that it is possible to have one's conscience "corrupted" (Titus 1:15 NIV) or defiled. Paul describes that defiled conscience as having been "seared as with a hot iron" (1 Timothy 4:2 NIV). The writer of Hebrews actually speaks of an "evil conscience" (Hebrews 10:22).

The conscience is one of our God-given internal faculties, a critical witness within us that tells us we ought to do what we believe to be right and not to do what we believe to be wrong. The conscience, however, does not instruct us as to what is right or wrong; it prods us to do what we have been taught is right.

It is therefore possible to be led astray by our conscience if we are deceived about what is right and what is wrong. It is important to understand that our conscience must be informed by the Word of God, by what it says is right and what it says is wrong. Without being shaped by the absolute standard of God's Word, our conscience is an unreliable guide for life because it is easily deceived and subject to emotions and moods.

Pastor D. Martyn Lloyd-Jones observed that present-day religion far too often soothes the conscience instead of awakening it and produces a sense of self-satisfaction and eternal safety rather than a sense of our unworthiness.[15]

Paul urges Timothy to hold "on to faith and a good conscience" (1 Timothy 1:19 NIV). And he goes on to tell his young protégé that a deacon in the church should be one who holds "the mystery of the faith with a pure conscience" (1 Timothy 3:9).

If we want our conscience to be our ally in holy

living, we must saturate it with God's Word and ask the Holy Spirit to convict us of sin and lead us in righteousness (Acts 23:1, 24:16; Romans 2:15, 9:1; 2 Corinthians 1:12; Hebrews 10:22, 13:18; 1 Peter 2:19, 3:16, 3:21).

The Breastplate of Righteousness

Put on the breastplate of righteousness.

EPHESIANS 6:14

What protection does the breastplate of righteousness provide?

The American Forces Press told of a soldier with the Army's 10th Mountain Division who was knocked down by small arms fire but got up and continued his mission. Hit again by enemy fire, the infantryman got up a second time and continued his mission. "He's still alive," said the news report, "thanks to the new Interceptor body armor being worn by soldiers and Marines." It weighs just sixteen pounds, compared to twenty-five pounds for the flak jacket, the previous body armor. Engineers are working to create an even lighter, stronger vest. "Our goal is to create a protective system that is lower profile, lower bulk, and lower weight," said one inventor. "We want it to be like a second skin, so the warfighter barely even knows that it's there, but that offers the protections needed in a combat environment."

When Paul says the well-dressed Christian soldier must wear the "breastplate of righteousness," he means that the righteousness of Christ should be like a second skin that will protect us from spiritual assaults by our enemy.

In one sense, of course, Christians are already equipped with the righteousness of Christ. We call this *positional* righteousness. According to 1 Corinthians 1:30, Christ *became* our righteousness, and when we trust Him as Savior, we are clothed in Him. Then, when God looks at us, He doesn't see us in our sins; He sees us clothed in the righteousness of Christ. That is our position before God.

But we must live out *practical* righteousness. We must commit ourselves to a life that is honest, upright, authentic, and full of integrity. When we find little ways of lying, cheating, and shading the truth, we give Satan a foothold in our hearts. Nothing so demoralizes and discourages a warrior as being involved in a spiritual battle, knowing there is a problem of character and integrity in his own life. The little sins we tolerate represent dangerous holes in our bulletproof vests. You can be sure that sooner or later, Satan will aim right at one of those spots.

We're in a battle, and our enemy is on the attack. We need to resist him. Satan can't stand the hymns of the faith, so sing! He can't overcome the prayers of the saints, so pray! He can't defeat the Lord Jesus Christ, so claim the power of Jesus' blood to defeat sin and Satan! He can't overthrow the truth, so quote the Scriptures! He can't vanquish the joy of the Lord, so rejoice! He can't divert God's grace, so use the shield of faith!

We must use the weapons God has given us. "Resist the devil and he will flee from you" (James 4:7). "Draw near to God and He will draw near to you" (v. 8).

> *It may be that Satan is planning some fresh temptation with which to assail you; but, though he desires to . . . sift you as wheat, Christ is praying for you, that your faith fail not.*
>
> CHARLES H. SPURGEON, IN HIS
> SERMON "THE TENSES"

What is the importance of righteousness in battle?

There is no power in a Christian's life if it is not a righteous life.

Apart from the righteousness we have in Christ, we have no defense against Satan's accusations. And every time we try to do battle with the enemy, he will go right for that weakness, bring to mind the sin in our lives, and perhaps even make us doubt our salvation. We won't be an effective witness because we'll think, *How can I tell them what Christ has done for me when my life is not any different from theirs?* Neither will we be victorious over temptation. Without righteousness, we are powerless to withstand Satan's tactics.

But the Christian who is wearing the breastplate of righteousness will go through life and, no matter what happens, will find some victory in every situation. In times of stress, in times of joy, in sorrow, in plenty, in want, there will be a consistent, godly quality about his or her life. That's what happens when you have the righteousness of Christ in you, and when you are outwardly living the righteousness of Christ.

What is sanctification?

The word *sanctification* means "to be set apart for a specific purpose." It is another way of looking at our journey with Christ, and it comes in three tenses—three dramatic dimensions.

Past sanctification happened the moment you said yes to Christ by accepting His offering of Himself on the cross as payment for your sins. When God forgave your sins, and you were washed by the blood of Christ, God declared that your debt was paid in full. He reserved a place for you in the heavenly places for eternity, and the Holy Spirit entered your heart. And that's just the past part!

Present sanctification is an ongoing growth process as, spiritual molecule by spiritual molecule, we are conformed to the image of Christ through the redeeming work of the Holy Spirit. Through prayer and by studying His Word, we become victors over issues in our lives as we become more like Christ. We learn to make decisions that honor Him and facilitate the Spirit's transformational work in our lives.

Then, most thrilling of all, there is *future sanctification.* There will be a day when we are finally freed from the presence of sin. As there can be no sin in heaven, no impurity in God's holy presence, sin must ultimately be eliminated. I can't imagine how wonderful it will be. The best definition of *sanctification* I've ever heard is this: "Becoming in practice what you already are in position." And what are Christians "in position"? We are clothed in the righteousness of Christ. Sanctification is the process of growing in holiness—living every day in light of who we are in Christ.

This is threefold sanctification. It began when I trusted Christ, and the penalty for my sin was removed by His death on my behalf. My sanctification continued as I began walking with the Lord, and I learned more and more how to be victorious over temptation and in trials. And my sanctification will be complete when Jesus takes me unto Himself in the future, when sin is judged and destroyed, and when eternal life begins for us. And that day, Paul tells us, "is nearer than when we first believed" (Romans 13:11).

> *In the way of righteousness is life, and in its pathway there is no death.*
>
> PROVERBS 12:28

How can I be consistent in righteousness?

The Bible teaches us that we are to cultivate righteousness in our lives until it becomes part of who we are. And I've had many Christians over the years tell me they get discouraged because they fail. Their Christian life is like a yo-yo, up and down, up and down.

The question then is, "How can I be righteous? Can I try harder?" Apparently, the apostle Paul attempted that approach. He decided to try harder, but he failed when he tried to be righteous in his own strength (Romans 7:15, 19). Someone might say, "Well, then, should I just give it up to God?" But how does that work? How can we become righteous by just passively waiting for it to happen to us?

The answer doesn't lie in either one of those strategies. Instead of trying to live better, we need to learn how to love better. We need to fall more deeply in love with God because that relation-ship will dictate our conduct. When we learn how to love the Lord through His Word and through prayer and fellowship and worship . . . when we practice the art of holiness . . . when we take time to be holy and love God with all our hearts . . . it will change our lives.

How can I know my heart is right?

The Bible says "where [our] treasure is, there [our] heart will be also" (Matthew 6:21). What this means is that our hearts dictate our lifestyles and define our priorities. Simply stated, our "treasure" indicates what is important to us.

Sometimes people wonder, *Is it okay if I do this? Can I get by with doing that?* But when we have thoughts like these, we are often just asking, How close can I get to the things of the world without getting in trouble with God? And when we do that, we are giving away our power to stand firm in spiritual battles (because of our separation from God). After all, when you really love somebody, you don't try to live as far away from that person as you can. You do everything possible to live as close as you can. This is the nature of love.

Some churches foster the idea that when you become a Christian, you "give up" the things of the world. But be assured, when you pursue the righteousness of Christ, the things that you hold dear, your "treasure," will inevitably change. The things that you once coveted will no longer appeal; they may even make you uncomfortable. When you walk away from the enticements of the world, you won't miss them, because God replaces them with something far better.

The Shoes of the Gospel of Peace

Stand therefore . . . having shod your feet with the preparation of the gospel of peace.

EPHESIANS 6:14–15

What protection do the shoes of the gospel of peace provide?

Roman soldiers wore special shoes for warfare: thick-soled, hobnailed sandals with wide leather straps. These sandals provided better traction during battle and gave soldiers a foundation that would protect their feet from injury and from traps set by the enemy.

So why did Paul say Christians should put on the shoes of the gospel of peace? As soldiers of Christ, we too must have solid footing for warfare—"the preparation of the gospel of peace." The word *preparation* comes from a Greek word that means "readiness" or "firmness." We must stand firm and trust that the One who has called us into battle will always be working for our good. If we spend our time worrying and fretting or questioning God's care and concern for us, we will be unproductive on the battlefield (Matthew 6:26–27).

The gospel of peace stabilizes our hearts because we know that God is on our side! He is working for our good! And the settled peace that only He can provide is our foundation for battle.

How do I arm myself with the shoes of the gospel of peace?

Believers are not in a battle against people but against the realm of devilish powers, so it's important to be equipped with the inner peace produced by the gospel of Christ. Paul says in Ephesians 2:14 that Christ is our peace: Jesus comes to us in the midst of the battle, when the struggle against temptation or the discouragements of life seem impossible, and He speaks peace to us. He gives the encouragement that keeps our morale up. That is the foundation on which we must fight—the shoes of peace.

How can we minister to others in this world of woe and warfare if our own hearts are so upset that we seem no different from anyone else? It's like going into battle barefoot, grimacing in pain as the rocks of anxiety press into our tender feet. Just as the right boots protect our soles, the peace of the gospel protects our souls. The good news of

Christ brings composure to our lives. It puts hard leather between us and the jagged stones of fear and doubt.

The Bible constantly tells us, "Do not fret . . . do not fear . . . do not let your hearts be troubled . . . do not be anxious . . . don't be discouraged." Are you going into your daily warfare shod with divine peace?

A great method to help you appropriate this peace in your life is Scripture memory. After all, Scripture is the Word of Peace. So when you get the Word of God in your life, you will find help to deal with the inevitable problems and stresses of life.

> *You will keep him in perfect peace, whose mind is stayed on You, because he trusts in You.*
> ISAIAH 26:3

As we grow in Christ, we grow in our ability to experience the peace of God.

What does it mean to let the peace of God "rule" in my heart?

Colossians 3:15 says we are to "let the peace of God rule in [our] hearts." In the language of the New Testament, the word *rule* is a word meaning "umpire." In other words, let the peace of God umpire your heart.

When you have a decision to make and you're walking with the Lord, one of the ways that you test your decision is by whether or not the Lord gives you peace about that decision. Have you ever heard someone say, "You know, I'd like to do this, but I just don't have peace about it"? I believe that God uses that sense of peace in our hearts to direct or confirm our decisions. That's how He rules in our hearts.

When you put on the shoes of peace, measure your life by the rule of peace and let its presence make a difference in your life.

The peace of God, which surpasses all understanding, will guard your hearts and minds through Christ Jesus.

PHILIPPIANS 4:7

"Peace I leave with you, My peace I give to you; not as the world gives do I give to you. Let not your heart be troubled."

JOHN 14:27

The Shield of Faith

Above all, [take] the shield of faith with which you will be able to quench all the fiery darts of the wicked one.

EPHESIANS 6:16

What protection does the shield of faith provide?

Roman battle shields were about four feet tall, two feet wide, and covered with thick leather and metal that could deflect incoming arrows. Those arrows were often tipped with leather, dipped in pitch, and lit on fire. The shield protected the soldiers from these flying, fiery darts.

For the Christian, the shield for battle is faith. In fact, faith is the key to all spiritual armor. And God gave faith to us to deflect the fiery darts of Satan—darts that have but one purpose, and that is to produce doubt, distress of mind, depression of spirit, and disappointment in relationships, in work, or in yourself. The shield of our faith in Christ is our defense (see Psalm 18:30; Proverbs 30:5; 1 John 5:4). And Scripture promises us that this shield is sufficient to repel even the enemy's best shot. Without that defense, however, we are very vulnerable: Satan knows where the joints and cracks are between our pieces of armor, and that's where he aims. If we are not protecting ourselves with the shield of faith, Satan can take us out. So, as the Bible says, "Above all, don't forget the shield!" It is a priority.

A shield of faith was definitely a priority for Reverend J. O. Fraser, a missionary to the Lisu people in China who labored on the China/Burma border for a number of years with no apparent success. Many men would have given up, but when he was discouraged, Fraser simply prayed and trusted—and kept working.

Here's what he wrote in his journal on January 16, 1916: "Not a single person at service in the morning. . . . The walls of Jericho fell down 'by faith.' Of all the instances of faith in Hebrews 11, this corresponds most nearly to my case."

Later, on February 5, after a day of fighting off the devil's darts of discouragement, he wrote: "I am not taking the black, despondent view I took yesterday. The opposition will not be overcome by reasoning or by pleading, but (chiefly) by steady, persistent prayer. . . . I am now setting my face like a flint: if the work seems to fail, then pray;

if services, etc., fall flat, then pray still more; if months slip by with little or no result, then pray still more and get others to help you."

Finally the long-awaited revival came like a dam burst, and to this day, the Lisu areas are among the most solidly Christian in China.

Why couldn't Satan defeat Fraser? The missionary held up the shield of faith. First John 5:4 (KJV) says, "This is the victory that overcometh the world, even our faith."

As for God, His way is perfect;
The word of the LORD is proven;
He is a shield to all who trust in Him.
                                        PSALM 18:30

How do I arm myself with the shield of faith?

In Galatians, Paul wrote, "I have been crucified with Christ; it is no longer I who live, but Christ lives in me; and the life which I now live in the flesh I live by faith in the Son of God, who loved me and gave Himself for me" (2:20).

Notice that Paul did not say, "I live my life in the flesh by *my* faith in the Son of God." No, it's not our faith; it is the faith that God gives us. Even our faith is a gift from God, our faith in Jesus Christ is our shield, and we are to "take up the shield of faith" (Ephesians 6:16 NIV).

Faith has to be appropriated before it can be used. The way we appropriate faith in our lives is by arming ourselves with the truth about God and who He is so that for every "fiery dart" Satan sends our way, we will have a solid answer, a relevant truth, or an applicable verse that we can use to resist him. We need to take what God has given us in the precious promises of His Word and mine from it the truths that will help us live the practical Christian life with victory. When we know what we believe, we are actively strengthening our shield of faith so that it will be impervious to any attack Satan sends our way.

What are the "fiery darts of the wicked one"?

Sometimes Satan, rightfully known as "the wicked one," attempts to destroy us by direct attack. He and his demons attack by shooting fiery darts at God's people. Sometimes Satan comes after us with a dart of discouragement; at other times he sends the dart of mistrust, telling us to doubt our own faith. Satan also sends darts of lust, lies, rumors, gossip, jealousies, covetousness, and temptations of all sorts. The devil has a quiver full of darts, and he sends exactly the right ones our way when we least expect it.

Satan wants to ruin our testimony and destroy our lives. But when we arm ourselves with the shield of faith, we are able to quench every dart Satan sends our way.

How can I join forces with other believers?

In Paul's day, Roman soldiers would lock their shields together and hunker down behind them as a defense against a rain of enemy arrows. Then, as they moved forward, the soldiers would use the linked shields as a defensive wall.

Author Stu Weber writes: "Do you see the critical point here? This is the shield of faith, which by design, is interlocked with the soldier next to you. This is the shield of faith utilized in community, the community of faith."[16]

The interlocking of shields is a picture of God's people coming together in church, in small groups, and in home groups to both withstand the enemy and help one another. We are to watch one another's back so that all of us are better protected from and prepared for the raining darts of the enemy.

For whatever is born of God overcomes the world. And this is the victory that has overcome the world—our faith.

1 JOHN 5:4

What can I do to strengthen my faith?

In order to fortify our faith, we must focus on the Object of our faith.

Our faith is not in faith itself. And the value of our faith is entirely dependent on the Object of our faith. Our faith is in the Lord God and His promises. The writer of the book of Hebrews tells us that we are to look "unto Jesus, the author and finisher of our faith" (Hebrews 12:2). We must keep our eyes on Christ, and we must not be lazy. We need to consistently exercise and practice an active faith.

God has given us everything we need to live a God-honoring life: the whole curriculum and all the notes. And we practice by taking what we know from the Word of God and putting it into operation. Step by step, we put together a life of obedience to the Word of God. That is what makes us strong and enables us to stand against the wiles of the enemy.

Take up the shield of faith!

The Helmet of
Salvation

Take the helmet of salvation.

Ephesians 6:17

What protection does the helmet of salvation provide?

The Roman soldier's helmet was obviously designed to protect his head, so it is easy to see the parallel helmet of salvation protecting the believer's mind from Satan's attacks.

But the helmet of salvation is more than simply knowing that you're a Christian. That is important, of course, but the helmet of salvation reaches far beyond the simple moment of salvation. It encompasses the whole scope of salvation—past, present, and future.

The enemy is constantly trying to wear down our defenses and corrupt our minds with temptation and rationalization and false teaching—anything to confuse our thinking about God and His purposes for our lives. Our only defense is to have the benefit of a mind that has lived in and conquered this world—and that is the mind of Christ. When we put on the helmet of salvation, we put on the mind of Christ and the wisdom of

God. Christ wants to equip us with His plans, His thoughts, His concepts, His truth, and His revelation. With Him, we can stand strong against Satan's furious attacks.

A key theme in the New Testament is that spiritual warfare is not fought like an earthly war "according to the flesh." Rather, "the weapons of our warfare are not carnal but mighty in God for pulling down strongholds, casting down arguments and every high thing that exalts itself against the knowledge of God, *bringing every thought into captivity to the obedience of Christ*" (2 Corinthians 10:3–5). Peter expressed a similar idea: "Always be ready to give a defense to everyone who asks you a reason for the hope that is in you" (1 Peter 3:15). A defense is a well-reasoned answer, and that means using the mind to repel untruths about God and about faith in Him.

The mind must be engaged if we are to resist Satan's attacks and promote and defend the faith. The primary battlefield for spiritual warfare is always the battlefield of the mind, where thoughts compete against one another. That's why we must fill our minds with the biblical defenses of the faith.

How do I arm myself with the helmet of salvation?

I believe that the mind is the most fiercely contested battleground in all of spiritual warfare. We have to guard our minds every moment to ensure that Satan does not slip in and plant seeds of carnal or sinful thinking. And in order to do that, the Bible says, we need God's helmet, His wisdom.

So how do we get God's wisdom? Paul says in 1 Corinthians 1:24 that Jesus Christ has become for us "the power of God and the wisdom of God." As we put on Jesus Christ, He becomes the wisdom of God to us.

Therefore, the helmet of salvation is the wisdom of God revealed in Christ. This wisdom is available to every believer through prayer and the reading of God's Word (James 1:5; 2 Timothy 3:15).

If any of you lacks wisdom, let him ask of God, who gives to all liberally and without reproach, and it will be given to him.

JAMES 1:5

What is wisdom?

Some Christians are operating with knowledge instead of wisdom. These individuals know a lot of facts about Christianity, but they lack the wisdom of God. The best definition of wisdom I have found is from the Old Testament scholar Tremper Longman. He wrote:

> Wisdom is the skill of living. It is a practical knowledge that helps one know how to act and how to speak in different situations. Wisdom entails the ability to avoid problems, and the skill to handle them when they present themselves. Wisdom includes the ability to interpret other people's speech and writing in order to react correctly to what they are saying to us.[17]

A simpler definition of wisdom is this: "doing the right thing without a precedent." The believer who can respond to an unexpected situation in the same way Christ would is someone who has biblical wisdom, who has the mind of Christ.

When wisdom enters your heart, and knowledge is pleasant to your soul, discretion will preserve you; understanding will keep you.
PROVERBS 2:10–11

Happy is the man who finds wisdom, and the man who gains understanding.
PROVERBS 3:13

[Wisdom] is more precious than rubies, and all the things you may desire cannot compare with her. Length of days is in her right hand, in her left hand riches and honor. Her ways are ways of pleasantness, and all her paths are peace. She is a tree of life to those who take hold of her, and happy are all who retain her.
PROVERBS 3:15–18

Wisdom is better than rubies, and all the things one may desire cannot be compared with her.
PROVERBS 8:11

In what way does the helmet of salvation prepare me for ministry?

When it comes to spiritual warfare, helmets are not optional. In fact, the helmet of salvation is a prerequisite to any kind of ministry because without our helmet—without God's wisdom—we're going to make a lot of mistakes and poor decisions.

In Acts 6:3 we read about the early church selecting the very first deacons. The disciples gave these instructions to their fellow believers: "Seek out from among you seven men of good reputation, full of the Holy Spirit and wisdom, whom we may appoint over this business." In other words, seek out men who are wearing their helmets of salvation, who walk in the wisdom of God.

In one of his letters, Paul reminds young Timothy of the source of his wisdom: "From childhood you have known the Holy Scriptures, which are able to make you wise for salvation through faith which is in Christ Jesus" (2 Timothy 3:15).

Do you know why Timothy was prepared to be a servant of God? His grandmother and his mother had taught him the Scriptures. Timothy was wearing his helmet; he knew the Holy Scriptures that were able to make him "wise for salvation." That knowledge of God's Word is what it takes to do the work of God.

What is my hope in the midst of combat?

The helmet of salvation is the promise of hope. As 1 Thessalonians 5:8 says, "Let us who are of the day be sober, putting on the breastplate of faith and love, and as a helmet the hope of salvation."

So what is our hope? It's the hope that Christ is ultimately going to resolve this warfare and that, one day, He will return and make all things new. We're fighting in a war that, in essence, we have already won. So even though the battle against Satan rages, we don't have to fear defeat. We know victory over sin is ours in Christ. So, we put on this helmet of salvation—this knowledge of what Jesus did—and the helmet of salvation is our hope in Christ.

In 1 Thessalonians 5:8, Paul refines the concept of the "helmet of salvation." There, he says Christians are to put on "as a helmet the hope of salvation." But in Scripture, salvation is not hope as the world uses the term. We are not merely wishing for Jesus to return in victory; our hope is unconditional and confident. Christian hope is a certainty.

How can I defend my faith in a world hostile to Christians?

This world is indeed hostile to the things of God. And there is a built-in conflict when a Christian lives in this world. Matthew 10:18–20 is an important passage in this regard:

> "You will be brought before governors and kings for My sake, as a testimony to them and to the Gentiles. But when they deliver you up, do not worry about how or what you should speak. For it will be given to you in that hour what you should speak; for it is not you who speak, but the Spirit of your Father who speaks in you."

This passage is not a license for avoiding Bible study, for merely opening your mouth and expecting God to speak through you. Instead, God promises here that when you are called to defend your faith, He will bring to your mind the words you need, words out of the storehouse of truth you have already committed to mind in your study.

Consider the apostles. They spoke far beyond their own natural ability—their wisdom and power often confounded their opponents.

As Christians, we are going to find ourselves on the defensive in this world, so we must be prepared to speak with the wisdom and power of Christ. We must be prepared to give an answer for the hope that lies within us (1 Peter 3:15). And that will happen only if we nurture our minds with God's truth, if we are students of His Word, and if we put on the helmet of salvation.

As Christians, we are going to find ourselves on the defensive in this world, so we must be prepared to speak with the wisdom and power of Christ.

How can I demolish Satan's strongholds in my heart and mind?

In the ancient world a stronghold was a fortress, a place where people could run for protection. We read that "The LORD is good, a stronghold in the day of trouble" (Nahum 1:7). But a stronghold can be a bad thing too. In spiritual warfare, a stronghold in the life of a Christian is a place where the enemy is entrenched—an established pattern, habit, or way of thinking that does not yet belong to God. And in each of our lives, Satan will seek to find some area of weakness where he can entrench himself and create havoc for us. But 2 Corinthians 10:4 tells us that we can use the armor of God to demolish those strongholds in our lives.

As we read the Scriptures and equip ourselves with the mind of Christ, with the helmet of salvation, God reveals to us those things in our lives that we have not yet given over to Him. And whether it's greed, pride, anger, addiction—whatever the stronghold—God will show us how, in the wisdom of Christ, to begin pulling it down by renewing our mind according to His Word (Romans 12:2).

What does it mean to "renew your mind"?

Your mind is Satan's target. The Bible could not be more clear: "I am afraid that just as Eve was deceived by the serpent's cunning, your minds may somehow be led astray from your sincere and pure devotion to Christ" (2 Corinthians 11:3 NIV).

Satan plays mind games with Christians using his craftiness. So we must renew our minds daily, "bringing every thought into captivity to the obedience of Christ" (2 Corinthians 10:5). That means we must be constantly programming our minds and our spirits with biblical truth and godly thoughts. Don't open yourself up to the ideas that can corrupt you.

Even though we will never reach perfection on this earth, we can determine, by the grace of God, to rework our mental diet so that the godly topics available to us will form the major portion of what we think about and meditate on. Listen to godly music that has lyrics that are uplifting and encouraging. Have God-centered conversations. Read literature that reflects Christian morality. Renew your mind.

The Sword of the Spirit

Take . . . the sword of the Spirit,
which is the word of God.

Ephesians 6:17

What protection does the sword of the Spirit provide?

Within God's armory we have only one offensive weapon to use in battle against the evil one—it is "the sword of the Spirit, which is the word of God" (Ephesians 6:17).

When Paul wrote to the Ephesians, he used the Greek word *machaira* for *sword*. He wasn't talking about what we would think of as a sword today; he was talking about a dagger, a weapon that people used in hand-to-hand combat. That metaphor suggests, then, that the sword of the Spirit . . . is a very precision-oriented instrument.[18] Specifically, the Word of God referred to in this passage is not the whole Bible (the *logos*) but a particular part of the Word, a promise (a *rhema*) to apply to a particular battle situation.

In other words, the Bible is an armory in which the individual swords of the Spirit are kept until you need them for close combat with the enemy. But unlike a material sword that you would use to pierce the body, the spiritual sword pierces the heart. A material sword gets duller as you use it, but a spiritual sword gets sharper every time you use it. And those spiritual swords are found within the covers of the Bible.

In Matthew 4, when Jesus was attacked by the tempter, He confronted Satan with three simple words: "It is written. . . ." And then Jesus quoted passages from Deuteronomy. Isn't it interesting that even the Lord Jesus, the Son of God, used the Scripture to defeat Satan?

Years ago my friend Swen Nater and I got together at a restaurant. We talked about the areas where we thought the enemy would come after us, and we took a concordance and researched the Scriptures. We came up with about forty "swords" for each of us, which we stored in the armories of our minds. I'd suggest you do the same. Think of areas in which you know Satan will tempt you, find some Bible verses relating to those areas, write them out on little cards, and put them where you will see them often. Memorize them. Internalize them. Learn them by heart—and be ready to use them when the enemy attacks.

Satan can't do much with people who assault him with Scripture.

How do I arm myself with the sword of the Spirit?

The Bible is an armory filled with swords of the Spirit, but most Christians visit the "New Armory" more than the "Old Armory." You might think there aren't many swords back in Leviticus, Numbers, or Deuteronomy that can help in battle today. But don't forget, when Jesus was tempted by Satan in the wilderness, all three of His swords were pulled from Deuteronomy (Matthew 4:1–11).

If we don't make a practice of reading and meditating on the entire Bible, we're going to miss a lot of good swords to use against the enemy. When we read, study, and meditate on the Word of God in its entirety, we'll have access to our choice of swords whenever we need one. But we have to know the inventory.

In other words, as believers, we need to memorize the Word of God because most of the temptations we face in life don't come while we have a Bible in our hands! But if we have committed Scripture to memory, we will be able to reach into our memory banks and pull out the exact swords we need to defeat the enemy.

Hebrews 4:12 presents a graphic portrayal of the power of the Word of God as a sword. Ancient double-edged swords were valuable because they cut both ways—on the down stroke and the back stroke. The sharpness of their points and blades ensured deep penetration into an enemy's body, even to the marrow, the innermost part of a human bone. Similarly, the Word of God is effective in all directions. Instead of separating joints and marrow, this sword goes to the heart of the soul and spirit. But like a soldier's sword, the Word of God is active only when it is taken up and used.

How can I effectively wield the sword of the Spirit?

In Matthew 4:1–11, we have an example of how Christ used three swords of the Spirit, three particular verses, to defeat the three temptations Satan presented in the wilderness.

TEMPTATION 1: Satan first tempted Jesus to turn stones into bread to satisfy His hunger. Remember, Jesus had been fasting for forty days. But Jesus never acted independently of the Father, nor did He ever perform a miracle to serve Himself. Instead, He took out a sword of the Spirit, Deuteronomy 8:3, and said to the enemy: "It is written, 'Man shall not live by bread alone, but by every word that proceeds from the mouth of God'" (Matthew 4:4).

TEMPTATION 2: Next, Satan tempted Jesus to prove He was the Son of God. Instead, Jesus pulled out another sword, Deuteronomy 6:16, and said: "It is written again, 'You shall not tempt the LORD your God'" (Matthew 4:7).

TEMPTATION 3: Satan told Jesus he would give Him the kingdoms of the world if He would fall down and worship him. But Jesus pulled out one final sword, Deuteronomy 6:13, and said, "Away with you, Satan! For it is written, 'You shall worship the LORD your God, and Him only you shall serve'" (Matthew 4:10).

Jesus resisted the devil with the Word of God, and "the devil left him" (v. 11). And we can use the sword of the Spirit just as Jesus did! All we have to do is reach into our armory and pull out the right sword. *It is written!*

Resist the devil and he will flee from you.
JAMES 4:7

How does the sword of the Spirit transform lives?

Author and preacher Haddon Robinson once wrote that "God speaks through the Bible. . . . Through the preaching of the Scriptures, God encounters men and women to bring them to salvation and to richness and ripeness in Christian character."[19]

Whether we are reading our Bibles, sitting in church, or listening to Christian radio, the sword of the Spirit can change us in a moment. That's the power of the Word of God! It is living and powerful, sharp enough to enable us to divide truth from falsehood and to discern divine realities from earthly lies (Hebrews 4:12).

That's why I get excited every time I preach the Word of God. When I am in the pulpit, I am throwing swords from the Bible. And I know that God can use those swords, those particular verses or promises from the Bible, to transform people's lives.

The word of God is living and powerful, and sharper than any two-edged sword, piercing even to the division of soul and spirit, and of joints and marrow, and is a discerner of the thoughts and intents of the heart.

HEBREWS 4:12

God's Armor

Be strong in the Lord and in the power
of His might. Put on the whole armor
of God, that you may be able to stand
against the wiles of the devil.

Ephesians 6:10–11

Am I always equipped with God's armor?

Spiritual armor is useful only if we put it on! If we are defeated in the warfare, if we are wounded in an unprotected place because we are without armor, it's not the fault of our Commander in Chief. God has given us everything we need to battle valiantly and victoriously in one Manual—the Bible. And the Bible doesn't say, "Wait for God to put it on you" but "Put it on yourself." It is the Christian's personal responsibility to appropriate the armor of God in his or her own life. This war is not something we fight as a group; every believer is involved in a personal battle with Satan. If we are not individually and personally implementing the armor of God, we are going to be victims instead of victors.

The armor is ready for us to put on—and we need to do that. We need to be continually arming ourselves for the warfare. Only then will we be prepared to go out and win the battles that will inevitably come against us.

Why do I need to put on the whole armor of God?

All six pieces of spiritual armor are necessary for every believer. No part of our lives can be left unprotected or exposed.

A pastor in Haiti told the following parable to illustrate for his people the fatal danger of having any part of our spiritual being exposed to the destructive powers of Satan:

A certain man wanted to sell his house for $2,000. Another man wanted very badly to buy it, but because he was poor, he couldn't afford the full price. After much bargaining, the owner agreed to sell the house for half the original price with just one stipulation: he would retain ownership of one small nail protruding from just over the door.

After several years, the original owner wanted the house back, but the new owner was unwilling to sell. So first the [original] owner went out, found the carcass of a dead dog, and hung it from the nail he still owned. Soon the house became unlivable, and the family was forced to sell the house to the owner of the nail.[20]

The Haitian pastor told his congregation, "If we leave the devil with even one small peg in our lives, he will return to hang his rotting garbage on it, making it unfit for Christ's habitation."[21]

That is the kind of ruthless enemy we're up against. Do not give him the tiniest toehold in your life. Do not open the door to your heart even a crack. Do not rationalize or excuse any failure to obey the true Lord of your life. And when failures or missteps occur—as they will—confess them immediately and be cleansed "from all unrighteousness" (1 John 1:9).

The only way to protect yourself from Satan's infiltration is to be on the side of the One who is more powerful than he is, the One who "is greater than he who is in the world" (1 John 4:4).

Put on the Lord Jesus Christ, and make no provision for the flesh, to fulfill its lusts.

ROMANS 13:14

How do I "put on" Christ?

Look again at the spiritual armor listed in Ephesians 6:14–17. Do you see that the armor is nothing less than Jesus Christ Himself? In fact, when Paul writes to the Romans, he says something very similar to what we find in Ephesians. He says in Romans 13:14, "Put on the Lord Jesus Christ."

In essence, Paul tells us that we are to wear Christ like we wear a suit of clothes.

Pastor and author Ray Stedman suggested this approach: "When I get up in the morning, I put on my clothes, intending them to be part of me all day, to go where I go and do what I do. They cover me and make me presentable to others. That is the purpose of clothes. In the same way, the apostle is saying to us, 'Put on Jesus Christ when you get up in the morning. Make Him a part of your life that day. Intend that He go with you everywhere you go, and that He acts through you in everything you do. Call upon His resources. Live your life *in Christ.*"[22]

The Warfare
of Prayer

[Pray] always with all prayer
and supplication in the Spirit . . .
with all perseverance and
supplication for all the saints.

Ephesians 6:18

What is the purpose of prayer in God's armory?

Every soldier needs a good communication device like a radio or a satellite phone. The same is true in spiritual warfare.

Paul ended his discussion on the armor God gives the Christian by saying, "[Pray] always with all prayer and supplication in the Spirit, being watchful to this end with all perseverance and supplication for all the saints" (Ephesians 6:18).

Praying always . . . all prayer . . . all perseverance . . . for all the saints. In other words, our radios should always be on. The batteries should always be charged. Our prayer lives should be strong, consistent, and sincere. Many battles can be won only on our knees. Perhaps the battle raging in your life is for a wayward child or a lost loved one. Perhaps the battle is to regain unity and peace in your church. Perhaps the battle is to overcome a bad habit or an addiction. Perhaps the battle is to break open a resistant mission field. The Bible says that the prayers of a righteous person are "powerful and effective" (James 5:16 NIV).

God intends us to be "more than conquerors" (Romans 8:37), but we can't successfully engage in spiritual warfare without spiritual weapons. We can't be strong in ourselves; we have to be strong in the Lord and in the power of His might. And we have to be dressed for battle.

Prayer is the energy that enables the warrior to wear the armor and wield the sword. No matter how talented we might be, if we try to fight spiritual battles in the energy of the flesh, we will never be victorious.

I asked for strength that I might achieve;
He made me weak that I might obey.
I asked for health that I might do great things;
He gave me grace that I might do better things.
I asked for riches that I might be happy;
He gave me poverty that I might be wise.
I asked for power that I might have the praise of men;
He gave me weakness that I might feel a need of God.
I asked for all things that I might enjoy life;
He gave me life that I might enjoy all things.
I received nothing I had asked for;
He gave me all that I had hoped for.[23]

Am I really to pray "always"? Is that even possible?

P raying always" . . . These words remind us of 1 Thessalonians 5:17, which says: "Pray without ceasing." That doesn't mean we constantly mutter prayers all day; it means that we, as soldiers, keep our two-way radios constantly on. We must keep the line open so that we can contact headquarters at a moment's notice. We're to be in continual communication with our Commander in Chief. Prayer isn't just something we do for a few minutes in the morning or evening. Instead, people of prayer talk to God all day and all night as needs and thoughts arise.

Clearly, this kind of praying is not based on emotion. We don't pray just when we feel particularly spiritual or passionate or needy. Rather, we live in the domain of prayer. It is part of the process of living a "sober . . . vigilant" life (1 Peter 5:8). Because our adversary, the devil, is constantly on the prowl for someone to devour, we must constantly be in prayer.

Be in communication with God all the time, in all circumstances, and in all places as if He were right beside you . . . because He is!

"Praying always with all prayer." According to this verse, we can—and we are called to—pray on any occasion, in any location, in any situation, and for any supplication. We can offer all kinds of prayers—praises, petitions, confessions, prayers of anguish and prayers of exaltation, long prayers and short prayers, individual prayers and group prayers. We can pray aloud and silently. We can write our prayers and sing our prayers. We can make prayer an exciting adventure rather than a boring routine.

"Praying always with all prayer and supplication." This word *supplication* means "asking God for what we need." James warned that we have not because we ask not (James 4:2). That's why we keep prayer lists, and that's why we share our prayer requests with others. Asking is the rule of the kingdom, for God has the resources to meet all our needs.

In the anonymous little book *The Kneeling Christian*, we read:

> Prayer is the key that unlocks the door of God's treasure-house. It is not too much to say that all real growth in the spiritual life—all victory over temptation, all confidence and peace in the presence of difficulties and dangers, all repose of spirit during times of great disappointment or loss, all habitual communion with God—depends on the practice of secret prayer.[24]

One of the first books on prayer I ever read was *Too Busy Not to Pray* by Bill Hybels. The title intrigued me; it sounded like an anomaly, a contradiction in terms. At the beginning of chapter 1, Hybels wrote this:

> Prayer is an unnatural activity. From birth we have been learning the rules of self-reliance as we strain and struggle to achieve self-sufficiency. Prayer flies in the face of those deep-seated values. It is an assault on human

autonomy, an indictment of independent living. To people in the fast lane, determined to make it on their own, prayer is an embarrassing interruption.[25]

For the Christian, prayer is where we receive our strength and comfort for each day—it is our connection with our Commander in Chief.

What does it mean to be "watchful" in prayer?

Paul's words in Ephesians 6:18 suggest that prayer requires care and diligence, that it is an extremely important dimension of the Christian life. Anything we "watch over" is of great importance to us. And, for believers, prayer definitely falls into that category.

A prayerful life does not consist of only the words we say to God. It begins long before we start to pray—it begins with the attitude of our hearts, the condition of our relationships with others, and the thoughts we meditate on during the day. The state of our prayer life reflects the state of our lives in general. We must permit nothing into our lives that would make us unfit for coming before God's "throne of grace" (Hebrews 4:16). The life of prayer is a watchful life in which we take care to avoid anything that would hinder our communication with God.

The root of the Greek word for *watchful* means "the absence of sleep due to remaining watchful for something—watching for an animal when hunting or watching for an enemy." The word signifies an alert, wakeful frame of mind, a requirement for someone who is guarding something as opposed to a casual, relaxed attitude. This attitude of watchfulness is key to and entirely consistent with the perspective needed by anyone engaged in spiritual warfare.

It's easy to find our mind wandering or find ourselves getting drowsy when we pray. I have found that I can pray much more alertly and carefully when I am outdoors, perhaps taking a walk, than when I'm on my knees. I do pray on my knees, but I can fight off sleep better by "prayer walking." Whatever we have to do to remain alert and watchful when we pray—we should do it. God wants the attention of our hearts and minds so that He can fill us with His strength as we engage in spiritual warfare.

Warriors must be vigilant in their prayer life, permitting nothing to disrupt it. Warriors guard their time, plan their schedule, nurture their prayer life, and guard against anything that will distract from or interfere with praying. I've found that reading a chapter from a book about prayer each day helps prepare my heart for praying. It's like priming the pump.

How does Satan attempt to derail my prayer life?

Prayer is an essential aspect of spiritual warfare. In fact, it is the lifeblood of those who seek to be victorious. And that's why Satan would like nothing better than to keep us from praying, so he sends us distractions, discouragement, delays, and disappointment. Satan is a master at deception and discouragement.

If, for instance, you have two productive days of watchful prayer, Satan might let you believe that you have finally mastered the discipline of prayer. Then, on the third day when you fail to be watchful in prayer, he will tell you that you're an utter failure, that you've completely blown it, and that there's no use trying any further. If you miss one day in fruitful prayer, Satan can try to convince you that you are beyond help and hope—that you needn't try again.

But the good news is, there's a secret to overcoming Satan's deception. As with any other area of the spiritual life, if you fail, the thing to do is to begin again. There is no permanent failure in learning to be a faithful disciple of Jesus. If you have a bad day in your prayer life, purpose to begin again! Don't give in to the devil's tactics that are designed specifically to keep you from praying.

The enemy of our souls wants to keep us from developing a relationship that he knows will bring joy and satisfaction to us. So, by the grace of God, we need to commit to keep on praying. Only in the process of praying will we find the meaning of life: a dynamic, personal relationship with the Creator, the living Lord, the Babe of Bethlehem, the Savior of the cross, the resurrection-morning Victor, the only One who is life to us.

A well-known Billy Graham story is about a woman who wrote that she had pleaded in prayer for ten years for the conversion of her husband but that he was more hardened than ever. Mr. Graham advised her to keep praying. One day he received another letter. The husband had been gloriously saved. "Suppose she had stopped after only ten years," said the evangelist. Then he added, "Never stop praying no matter how dark and hopeless your case may seem."

Prayer is an essential aspect of
SPIRITUAL WARFARE.
In fact, it is the lifeblood of those who seek to be victorious.

What does it mean to be a "prayer warrior"?

Prayer is work—and it requires an all-out battle. Prayer is not an idle pastime or an optional exercise reserved for the "more spiritual" believers. Prayer is the hard-work business of the church of Jesus Christ. The kind of prayer that changes hearts . . . and transforms neighborhoods . . . and rebuilds communities . . . and revives nations is intense, fervent, and all business. It takes a proactive commitment on our part to set aside the time and effort to be strong in prayer and to give energy to our praying. Colossians 4:2 says we are to "continue earnestly in prayer." That's what it means to be a prayer warrior. Fierce hand-to-hand combat with issues of daily living, fought in God's strength and by His grace—that is what committed Christian prayer looks like.

I've learned that Satan trembles when he sees the least of God's children on their knees. Praise given to God causes the enemy to be incredibly uncomfortable. Whatever evil the devil wants to do, his plan is much more difficult to complete when God's people are praying.

How can I know
what to pray for?

There is no secret to answered prayer, but there is an important guideline—we are to pray according to God's will. And how can we know what to pray? The answer is . . . by the indwelling Holy Spirit.

The same Holy Spirit who inspired the writing of the Word of God lives in every born-again follower of Christ. The Spirit helps shape our prayers to be in accordance with the will and Word of God (Romans 8:26–27). As we saturate our minds and hearts with the Word of God, we grow in our sense of what His will is. Just as a child learns what things to ask or not ask of his or her father, so we learn how to ask according to our Father's will. And when a situation is too complex or we are overwhelmed, the Spirit comes alongside to help us pray when we are unsure or cannot find the words.

Recently I read these words about prayer written by pastor and author Alan Redpath: "Before we can pray, 'Thy Kingdom come,' we must be willing to pray—'My kingdom go!'"[26]

He who searches the hearts knows what the mind of the Spirit is, because He makes intercession for the saints according to the will of God.

ROMANS 8:27

Is there a model for prayer?

God longs for His people to communicate with Him, to talk to Him in the same way we would speak with the most precious person in our life. God doesn't want vain repetitions; He wants real communication (Matthew 6:7). Jesus teaches us to approach God honestly, openly, and sincerely. There are no special words we must use before we're allowed into God's presence. Yet, if we are to pray effectively, there are some key ideas to keep in mind, and that's what the Lord's Prayer is all about.

The Lord's Prayer (Matthew 6:9–13) is a model for us to follow in our prayer lives. If we get this remarkable prayer down deep into our hearts and minds where it belongs, it will change our lives. It wasn't created to make us feel guilty or unworthy but to show us the proper and most effective way to enter the very throne room of God Almighty.

Incredible as it may seem, God is waiting to

hear from us. He wants us to come boldly into His presence. And this prayer shows us the way.

"Our Father in heaven, hallowed be Your name. Your kingdom come. Your will be done on earth as it is in heaven. Give us this day our daily bread. And forgive us our debts, as we forgive our debtors. And do not lead us into temptation, but deliver us from the evil one. For Yours is the kingdom and the power and the glory forever. Amen."

MATTHEW 6:9–13

How can I develop an effective prayer life?

I t's one thing to be told to do something; it's even more helpful to be shown how to do it. But the best way to learn anything is by practicing it ourselves. The best way to learn to pray as Jesus taught is to start praying today—using the pattern of the Lord's Prayer in Matthew 6.

The Lord's Prayer is arguably the most famous prayer in the world. Perhaps, however, it should more accurately be called the "Disciples' Prayer" since the prayer asks for forgiveness of sins—and we know Christ never sinned. It is the Lord's Prayer because Jesus taught it, not because He prayed it for Himself.

There are just sixty-six words in this prayer, but it has been the basis of countless sermons, books, and even songs. Pastor Andrew Murray once said, "It is a form of prayer that becomes the model and the inspiration for all other prayers, and yet always draws us back to itself as the deepest utterance of our souls before God."

The Lord's Prayer is perfectly balanced. It teaches us to look first to God, then to ourselves. It teaches us to forgive and receive forgiveness. And it teaches us to depend wholly upon God for everything.

The Lord did not give us this prayer so that we would memorize it and repeat it as a mindless ritual. Jesus gave us this prayer as an outline to follow when we pray.

Several years ago I organized this prayer—based on Jesus' example—to use in my own prayer life, and I include this outline to encourage you to pray as our Lord has taught us to pray.

PRACTICAL APPLICATION OF THE DISCIPLES' PRAYER

Matthew 6:5–15

Perspective

Before I start the journey, I have decided . . .

Not to pray like the hypocrites: "They love to pray . . . that they may be seen by men" (Matthew 6:5).

Not to pray like the heathen: "They think that they will be heard for their many words" (Matthew 6:7).

Praise

"Our Father which art in heaven, Hallowed be thy name" (Matthew 6:9 KJV).

"Enter into His gates with thanksgiving, and into His courts with praise" (Psalm 100:4).

I Will Hallow His Name By . . .

Rehearsing His Names

- *Jehovah-Tsidkenu*, Jehovah Our Righteousness (Jeremiah 23:6)
- *Jehovah-Mekaddishkhem*, Jehovah Who Sanctifies (Leviticus 20:7–8)
- *Jehovah-Shalom*, Jehovah Who Is Our Peace (Judges 6:24)
- *Jehovah-Shammah*, Jehovah Is There (Ezekiel 48:35)
- *Jehovah-Rophe*, The Lord Who Heals (Exodus 15:26)
- *Jehovah-Jireh*, The Lord Will Provide (Genesis 22:14)

- *Jehovah-Nissi,* The Lord Is My Banner (Exodus 17:15)
- *Jehovah-Roi,* The Lord Who Is My Shepherd (Psalm 23:1)

Respecting His Greatness: His Attributes

- Eternal (Psalm 90:2)
- Unchanging (Malachi 3:6)
- Holy (Psalm 99:3)
- Love (1 John 4:8)
- All-powerful (Revelation 19:6)
- All-knowing (Acts 15:18)
- Ever-present (Psalm 139:7–11)
- Righteous (Psalm 11:7)
- Sovereign (Ephesians 1:11)
- True (John 17:3)
- Faithful (Lamentations 3:23)
- Good (Matthew 19:17)
- Kind (Psalm 31:21)
- Longsuffering (Psalm 86:15)

Recognizing His Presence

"I have set the LORD always before me" (Psalm 16:8).

Priorities

"Thy kingdom come, Thy will be done in earth, as it is in heaven" (Matthew 6:10 KJV).

"Seek first the kingdom of God and His righteousness, and all these things shall be added to you" (Matthew 6:33).

I Will Remember That . . .

1. I am a Person—I have a relationship with God.
2. I am a Partner—I have a relationship with my spouse.
3. I am a Parent—I have a relationship with my children.
4. I am a Provider—I have a responsibility in my job/profession.
5. I am a Participant—I have a responsibility in other things I am asked to do.

Provision

"Give us this day our daily bread" (Matthew 6:11 KJV).

"Ask, and it will be given to you; seek, and you will find; knock, and it will be opened to you" (Luke 11:9).

1. I will depend on God for my needs (Psalm 104:27; James 1:17).
2. I will distinguish between needs and wants:

   - "Our daily bread" (1 Timothy 6:8)
   - Something to put on: clothes
   - Something to put in: food
   - Something to put over: shelter

3. I will discipline myself not to worry.
   "Give us . . . our daily bread." Day to day, not week to week, or month to month, or year to year.
4. I will defer to the needs of others.
   "Give us," not *me*. "Give us our," not *my*.

Personal Relationships

"And forgive us our debts, as we forgive our debtors" (Matthew 6:12 KJV).

"For if you forgive men their trespasses, your heavenly Father will also forgive you. But if you do not forgive men their trespasses, neither will your Father forgive your trespasses" (Matthew 6:14–15).

1. We are to forgive because we are forgiven. Matthew 18:21–35 explains the importance of forgiving one another.
2. We are to forgive just as we are forgiven (Ephesians 4:32).
3. We are to forgive in order that we might be forgiven (Psalm 66:18).
4. We are to forgive before we need to be forgiven.

   At the start of each day, we remember our forgiveness and determine to forgive those who will hurt us.
5. We are to forgive always—and it is always our turn.

   How often? (Matthew 18:22)

   Who initiates? (Matthew 18:35; Mark 11:25)

Protection

"And lead us not into temptation, but deliver us from evil" (Matthew 6:13 KJV).

Six Steps of Temptation

1. Deceit
2. Delight
3. Desire

4. Deliberation
5. Defeat
6. Despair

Overcoming Temptation

1. Fight (James 4:7)
2. Follow (James 4:8)
3. Flee (2 Timothy 2:22; Romans 13:14)
4. Feed (Psalm 119:11)

Deliverance from Evil

- Deliverance from persecution (Psalm 22:19).
- Deliverance from peril (Psalm 31:1–2, 15).
- Deliverance from problems (Psalm 34:4, 17).

"The Lord knows how to deliver the godly out of temptations" (2 Peter 2:9).

Praise Again

"For thine is the kingdom, and the power, and the glory, forever. Amen" (Matthew 6:13 KJV).

- Lord, I praise You for Your sovereignty.
  "Thine is the kingdom . . ."
- Lord, I praise You for Your authority.
  "And the power . . ."

- Lord, I praise You for Your majesty.
  "And the glory . . ."
- Lord, I praise You for Your eternality.
  "Forever."

  Amen.

Why should I continue to pray when I feel God isn't answering my prayers?

We err when we judge the effectiveness or importance of our prayers solely by what we can see happening around us.

Prayer is a matter of faith. Prayer is taking God at His word and understanding God's promise that, if we pray, He will hear and respond. We must keep on praying even when we cannot see what He is doing.

We do not see into the world in which God lives, but He definitely sees into ours. By praying, we give evidence that we have committed ourselves to Him, that we take God at His word, that we trust Him, and that even though we can't always see what He is doing, we know He is working in our lives.

He shall call upon Me, and I
will answer him; I will be with
him in trouble; I will deliver
him and honor him. With long
life I will satisfy him, and show
him My salvation.

Psalm 91:15–16

What are some ways I can pray for others?

In Ephesians 6:18, Paul's admonition about the importance of prayer is to pray "for all the saints." Every Christian is included in "all the saints."

If we compare how Paul prayed for people with how we pray for others, we might be surprised. Oftentimes we pray for someone to be healed of a sickness, find a good job, have a safe vacation, restore a relationship, and so on—things that have to do with our personal needs as individuals. Our prayers tend to be focused on the material, physical aspects of life. That's not to say God isn't concerned about the daily events that affect our lives, because He is, but we cannot overlook the importance of praying for spiritual wisdom as well.

Knowing that, the apostle Paul prayed continually for the saints in the churches he founded and ministered to, and when he prayed, he focused on the spiritual aspects of life. He prayed for increased love, power, discernment, and knowledge of God's will—the very things Satan would attempt to take away from Christians in order to confuse, weaken, or discourage us (Ephesians 1:18–19, 3:16–19; Philippians 1:9–11; Colossians 1:9; 1 Thessalonians 3:11–13; 2 Thessalonians 2:16–17).

As we pray for "all the saints," let's remember to pray for these deeper spiritual realities. That is where spiritual warfare is going to be either won or lost.

Strategic warfare prayer needs a place, a purpose, a plan—but most of all, someone to pray.

How can I persevere in the battle when I'm afraid?

I know what it's like to have a "fear day." Sometimes, suddenly and out of nowhere, the spirit of fear grips my heart, and I have to drop everything and tell God about my fear, asking Him to deliver me from it.

Fear is paralyzing. Fear can keep us from doing the things God wants us to do. That's why Jesus tells us to pray for deliverance from evil. When fear strikes, give it to God with a simple prayer: "Lord, deliver me from evil, including all my fear. This situation is beyond me. I can't cope with it. But You can. Please extend Your hand, and by Your power, help me and deliver me."

Whenever I am afraid, I will trust in You.

Psalm 56:3

God is my salvation, I will trust and not be afraid; "for Yah, the Lord, is my strength and song; He also has become my salvation."

ISAIAH 12:2

Conclusion

How should I live today in light of the spiritual battle before me?

Day by day the battle is heating up, and the challenges are becoming greater; but we're not in doubt as to how it's going to turn out. God has given us a hope that is secure, that is steadfast, and that can never be touched. Our hope is beyond decay or destruction. Because Jesus Christ is eternal, our hope in Him is eternal. And we can live in hope if we understand and believe the truth concerning the risen Christ. We have a living hope, a hope based upon what Jesus Christ did when He arose from the grave. He gained victory over death.

By virtue of that accomplishment, Jesus has laid claim to our faith and says in effect, "If I came out of the grave victorious over death, and you put your trust in Me, you can know that same victory—not only over sin and death, but in your life, day by day."

We are victors through Christ! We just need to start acting like it. We are God's people, and Satan does not have any claim to us unless we give it to him. And the way we keep that from happening is by putting on the whole armor of God every day so that we might be able to stand against the evil one and "having done all, to stand."

Take up the whole armor of God, that you may be able to withstand in the evil day, and having done all, to stand.

EPHESIANS 6:13

The Warrior's Prayer

The precision of "The Warrior's Prayer" will help you to put on each piece of spiritual armor with purpose and to start each day in communion with God. When we remain persistent and focused in prayer, our eyes begin to open to the power of Christ in our lives, and we become armed for victory!

Heavenly Father,
Your warrior prepares for battle.
Today I claim victory over Satan by putting on
the whole armor of God!
I put on the Girdle of Truth!
May I stand firm in the truth of Your Word
so I will not be a victim of Satan's lies.
I put on the Breastplate of Righteousness!
May it guard my heart from evil
so I will remain pure and holy,

protected under the blood of Jesus Christ.
I put on the Shoes of Peace!
May I stand firm in the Good News of the Gospel
so Your peace will shine through me
and be a light to all I encounter.
I take the Shield of Faith!
May I be ready for Satan's fiery darts of
doubt, denial, and deceit
so I will not be vulnerable to spiritual defeat.
I put on the Helmet of Salvation!
May I keep my mind focused on You
so Satan will not have a stronghold in my
thoughts.
I take the Sword of the Spirit!
May the two-edged sword of Your Word
be ready in my hands
so I can expose the tempting words of Satan.
By faith Your warrior has put on
the whole armor of God!
I am prepared to live this day in spiritual victory!
Amen.

Spiritual Warfare
Reference Guide

- DEUTERONOMY 20:1 When you go out to battle against your enemies, and see horses and chariots and people more numerous than you, do not be afraid of them; for the LORD your God is with you, who brought you up from the land of Egypt.

- 2 SAMUEL 22:3–4 The God of my strength, in whom I will trust; my shield and the horn of my salvation, my stronghold and my refuge; my Savior, You save me from violence. I will call upon the Lord, who is worthy to be praised; so shall I be saved from my enemies.

- PSALM 27:3 Though an army may encamp against me, my heart shall not fear; though war may rise against me, in this I will be confident.

- PSALM 44:5 Through You we will push down our enemies; through Your name we will trample those who rise up against us.

- PSALM 46:1–2 God is our refuge and strength, a very present help in trouble. Therefore we will not fear, even though the earth be removed, and though the mountains be carried into the midst of the sea.

- PSALM 60:11–12 Give us help from trouble, for the help of man is useless. Through God we will do valiantly, for it is He who shall tread down our enemies.

- PSALM 121:7–8 The LORD shall preserve you from all evil; He shall preserve your soul. The LORD shall preserve your going out and your coming in from this time forth, and even forevermore.

- PROVERBS 25:28 Whoever has no rule over his own spirit is like a city broken down, without walls.

- ISAIAH 41:10 "Fear not, for I am with you; be not dismayed, for I am your God. I will strengthen you, yes, I will help you, I will uphold you with My righteous right hand."

- ISAIAH 54:17 "No weapon formed against you shall prosper, and every tongue which rises against you in judgment you shall condemn. This is the heritage of the servants of the Lord, and their righteousness is from Me," says the Lord.

- MATTHEW 6:13 "And do not lead us into temptation, but deliver us from the evil one. For Yours is the kingdom and the power and the glory forever. Amen."

- MATTHEW 18:18 "Assuredly, I say to you, whatever you bind on earth will be bound in heaven, and whatever you loose on earth will be loosed in heaven."

- LUKE 10:19 "Behold, I give you the authority to trample on serpents and scorpions, and over all the power of the enemy, and nothing shall by any means hurt you."

- JOHN 10:10 "The thief does not come except to steal, and to kill, and to destroy. I have come that they may have life, and that they may have it more abundantly."

- JOHN 16:33 "These things I have spoken to you, that in Me you may have peace. In the world you will have tribulation; but be of good cheer, I have overcome the world."

- ROMANS 8:5–6 For those who live according to the flesh set their minds on the things of the flesh, but those who live according to the Spirit, the things of the Spirit. For to be carnally minded is death, but to be spiritually minded is life and peace.

- ROMANS 8:31 What then shall we say to these things? If God is for us, who can be against us?

- ROMANS 8:35 Who shall separate us from the love of Christ? Shall tribulation, or distress, or persecution, or famine, or nakedness, or peril, or sword?

- ROMANS 8:38–39 For I am persuaded that neither death nor life, nor angels nor principalities nor powers, nor things present nor things to come, nor height nor depth, nor any other created thing, shall be able to separate us from the love of God which is in Christ Jesus our Lord.

- ROMANS 12:2 And do not be conformed to this world, but be transformed by the renewing of your mind, that you may prove what is that good and acceptable and perfect will of God.

- ROMANS 12:21 Do not be overcome by evil, but overcome evil with good.

- 1 CORINTHIANS 15:57 But thanks be to God, who gives us the victory through our Lord Jesus Christ.

- 1 CORINTHIANS 16:13 Watch, stand fast in the faith, be brave, be strong.

- 2 CORINTHIANS 1:3–4 Blessed be the God and Father of our Lord Jesus Christ, the Father of mercies and God of all comfort, who comforts us in all our tribulation, that we may be able to comfort those who are in any trouble, with the comfort with which we ourselves are comforted by God.

- 2 CORINTHIANS 4:3–4 But even if our gospel is veiled, it is veiled to those who are perishing, whose minds the god of this age has blinded, who do not believe, lest the light of the gospel of the glory of Christ, who is the image of God, should shine on them.

- 2 CORINTHIANS 7:1 Therefore, having these promises, beloved, let us cleanse ourselves from all filthiness of the flesh and spirit, perfecting holiness in the fear of God.

- 2 CORINTHIANS 10:3–5 For though we walk in the flesh, we do not war according to the flesh. For the weapons of our warfare

are not carnal but mighty in God for pulling down strongholds, casting down arguments and every high thing that exalts itself against the knowledge of God, bringing every thought into captivity to the obedience of Christ.

- GALATIANS 5:17 For the flesh lusts against the Spirit, and the Spirit against the flesh; and these are contrary to one another, so that you do not do the things that you wish.

- GALATIANS 5:24–25 And those who are Christ's have crucified the flesh with its passions and desires. If we live in the Spirit, let us also walk in the Spirit.

- EPHESIANS 4:26–27 "Be angry, and do not sin": do not let the sun go down on your wrath, nor give place to the devil.

- EPHESIANS 6:10–11 Finally, my brethren, be strong in the Lord and in the power of His might. Put on the whole armor of God, that you may be able to stand against the wiles of the devil.

- EPHESIANS 6:12–13 For we do not wrestle against flesh and blood, but against principalities, against powers, against the rulers of the darkness of this age, against spiritual hosts of wickedness in the heavenly places. Therefore take up the whole armor of God, that you may be able to withstand in the evil day, and having done all, to stand.

- EPHESIANS 6:14–17 Stand therefore, having girded your waist with truth, having put on the breastplate of righteousness, and having shod your feet with the preparation of the gospel of peace; above all, taking the shield of faith with which you will be able to quench all the fiery darts of the wicked one. And take the helmet of salvation, and the sword of the Spirit, which is the word of God.

- COLOSSIANS 1:13 He has delivered us from the power of darkness and conveyed us into the kingdom of the Son of His love.

- COLOSSIANS 2:15 Having disarmed principalities and powers, He made a public spectacle of them, triumphing over them in it.

- 2 THESSALONIANS 3:3 But the Lord is faithful, who will establish you and guard you from the evil one.

- 1 TIMOTHY 6:12 Fight the good fight of faith, lay hold on eternal life, to which you were also called and have confessed the good confession in the presence of many witnesses.

- 2 TIMOTHY 1:7 For God has not given us a spirit of fear, but of power and of love and of a sound mind.

- 2 TIMOTHY 4:18 And the Lord will deliver me from every evil work and preserve me for His heavenly kingdom. To Him be glory forever and ever. Amen!

- JAMES 1:2–4 My brethren, count it all joy when you fall into various trials, knowing that the testing of your faith produces patience. But let patience have its perfect work, that you may be perfect and complete, lacking nothing.

- JAMES 4:7–8 Therefore submit to God. Resist the devil and he will flee from you. Draw near to God and He will draw near to you. Cleanse your hands, you sinners; and purify your hearts, you double-minded.

- 1 PETER 4:16 Yet if anyone suffers as a Christian, let him not be ashamed, but let him glorify God in this matter.

- 1 PETER 5:8–9 Be sober, be vigilant; because your adversary the devil walks about like a roaring lion, seeking whom he may devour. Resist him, steadfast in the faith, knowing that the same sufferings are experienced by your brotherhood in the world.

- 1 JOHN 4:4 You are of God, little children, and have overcome them, because He who is in you is greater than he who is in the world.

- 1 JOHN 5:19 We know that we are of God, and the whole world lies under the sway of the wicked one.

Prayer Reference Guide

- 2 CHRONICLES 7:14 "If My people who are called by My name will humble themselves, and pray and seek My face, and turn from their wicked ways, then I will hear from heaven, and will forgive their sin and heal their land."

- PSALM 4:1 Hear me when I call, O God of my righteousness! You have relieved me in my distress; have mercy on me, and hear my prayer.

- PSALM 6:8–10 Depart from me, all you workers of iniquity; for the LORD has heard the voice of my weeping. The LORD has heard my supplication; the LORD will receive my prayer. Let all my enemies be ashamed and greatly troubled; let them turn back and be ashamed suddenly.

- PSALM 18:3 I will call upon the LORD, who is worthy to be praised; so shall I be saved from my enemies.

- PSALM 55:16 As for me, I will call upon God, and the LORD shall save me.

- PSALM 61:1–2 Hear my cry, O God; attend to my prayer. From the end of the earth I will cry to You, when my heart is overwhelmed; lead me to the rock that is higher than I.

- PSALM 118:5 I called on the LORD in distress; the LORD answered me and set me in a broad place.

- PSALM 145:18 The LORD is near to all who call upon Him, to all who call upon Him in truth.

- PROVERBS 15:29 The LORD is far from the wicked, but He hears the prayer of the righteous.

- MATTHEW 5:44 "But I say to you, love your enemies, bless those who curse you, do good to those who hate you, and pray for those who spitefully use you and persecute you."

- MATTHEW 26:41 "Watch and pray, lest you enter into temptation. The spirit indeed is willing, but the flesh is weak."

- MARK 11:24 "Therefore I say to you, whatever things you ask when you pray, believe that you receive them, and you will have them."

- MARK 14:38 "Watch and pray, lest you enter into temptation. The spirit indeed is willing, but the flesh is weak."

- LUKE 21:36 "Watch therefore, and pray always that you may be counted worthy to escape all these things that will come to pass, and to stand before the Son of Man."

- ROMANS 12:12 Rejoicing in hope, patient in tribulation, continuing steadfastly in prayer.

- EPHESIANS 6:18 Praying always with all prayer and supplication in the Spirit, being watchful to this end with all perseverance and supplication for all the saints.

- PHILIPPIANS 4:6–7 Be anxious for nothing, but in everything by prayer and supplication, with thanksgiving, let your requests be made known to God; and the peace of God, which surpasses all understanding, will guard your hearts and minds through Christ Jesus.

- COLOSSIANS 1:9 For this reason we also, since the day we heard it, do not cease to pray for you, and to ask that you may be filled with the knowledge of His will in all wisdom and spiritual understanding.

- COLOSSIANS 4:2 Continue earnestly in prayer, being vigilant in it with thanksgiving.

- 1 THESSALONIANS 5:16–18 Rejoice always, pray without ceasing, in everything give thanks; for this is the will of God in Christ Jesus for you.

- 2 THESSALONIANS 3:1–2 Finally, brethren, pray for us, that the word of the

Lord may run swiftly and be glorified, just as it is with you, and that we may be delivered from unreasonable and wicked men; for not all have faith.

- HEBREWS 5:7 In the days of His flesh, when He had offered up prayers and supplications, with vehement cries and tears to Him who was able to save Him from death, and was heard because of His godly fear.

- JAMES 5:13 Is anyone among you suffering? Let him pray. Is anyone cheerful? Let him sing psalms.

- 1 JOHN 5:14 Now this is the confidence that we have in Him, that if we ask anything according to His will, He hears us.

- JUDE 1:20 But you, beloved, building yourselves up on your most holy faith, praying in the Holy Spirit.

Additional Resources from Dr. David Jeremiah

What Are You Afraid Of?

Fear often arises involuntarily in the face of unwanted circumstances. For many people, worry and anxiety keep them from the life God has called them to. But fear can be overcome through faith in our heavenly Father. In *What Are You Afraid Of?* Dr. Jeremiah discusses nine fears we should *overcome* along with one fear we should *embrace*—the fear of God.

Slaying the Giants in Your Life

Giants—fear, loneliness, worry, doubt—plague many people in our world today. These giants cause many Christians to stumble or fall away from God's path. In *Slaying the Giants in Your Life*, Dr. Jeremiah uses real-life stories to show you God's promise of protection so that you can slay the giants in your life.

Living with Confidence in a Chaotic World
Our world is filled with chaos. Natural disasters and moral depravity are on the rise, and violence happens all around us. So what do we do now? In *Living with Confidence in a Chaotic World*, Dr. Jeremiah brings us hope through God's Word by helping us stay centered on Christ.

Overcoming Loneliness
Nobody is exempt from the pain loneliness brings. Some even feel its physical effects in the pit of their stomach. Whatever the effect, we are all susceptible to loneliness. In this book, Dr. Jeremiah suggests ways to help you heal and provides reassurance that God is there, helping you overcome your loneliness.

About Dr. David Jeremiah

Dr. David Jeremiah serves as senior pastor of Shadow Mountain Community Church in El Cajon, California. He is the founder and host of *Turning Point*, a ministry committed to providing Christians with sound Bible teaching relevant to today's changing times through radio and television, the Internet, live events, and resource materials and books. A best-selling author, Dr. Jeremiah has written more than fifty books, including *Captured by Grace, Living with Confidence in a Chaotic World, What in the World Is Going On?, The Coming Economic Armageddon, God Loves You: He Always Has—He Always Will,* and *What Are You Afraid Of?*

Dr. Jeremiah's commitment to teaching the complete Word of God continues to make him a sought-after speaker and writer. His passion for reaching the lost and encouraging believers in their faith is demonstrated through his faithful communication of biblical truths.

A dedicated family man, Dr. Jeremiah and his wife, Donna, have four grown children and twelve grandchildren.

Notes

1. J. C. Ryle, *Holiness* (Chicago: Moody), 115.
2. Alfred J. Hough, "Don't Believe in a Devil" (1889, Public Domain).
3. Stu Weber, *Spirit Warriors* (Colorado Springs: Multnomah Books, 2003), 172.
4. John Phillips, *Exploring Ephesians and Philippians: An Expository Commentary* (Grand Rapids, MI: Kregel Publications, 1995), 187.
5. Ryle, *Holiness*, 115.
6. Ibid., 118.
7. Sun Tzu, *The Art of War* (Hollywood, FL: Simon and Brown, 2010), 11.
8. Terry Law, *The Truth About Angels* (Lake Mary, FL: Charisma House, 2006), 126.
9. C. S. Lewis, *Mere Christianity* (San Francisco: HarperCollins, 1952), 121.
10. D. Martyn Lloyd-Jones, *The Christian Warfare* (Grand Rapids, MI: Baker Book House, 1977), 20–21.
11. R. Kent Hughes, *Ephesians: The Mystery of the Body of Christ* (Wheaton, IL: Crossway, 1990), 217.
12. John Calvin, from *The Institutes of Christian Religion*, Book 1, chapters 14 and 18.
13. William Manchester, *The Last Lion: Winston Spencer*

Churchill: Alone, 1932–1940 (New York: Bantam Books, 2013), 171.

14. Roger Olson, *The Story of Christian Theology* (Downers Grove, IL: InterVarsity Press, 1999), 20–21.

15. Lloyd-Jones, *The Christian Warfare*, 21.

16. Weber, *Spirit Warriors*, 172.

17. Tremper Longman, *How to Read Proverbs* (Downers Grove, IL: InterVarsity Press, 2002), 14.

18. John MacArthur, *How to Meet the Enemy: Arming Yourself for Spiritual Warfare* (Colorado Springs: Victor Books, 1992), 141.

19. Haddon Robinson, *Biblical Preaching* (Grand Rapids, MI: Baker Books, 2001), 20.

20. Craig Brian Larson, *Leadership Journal* and *750 Engaging Illustrations for Preachers, Teachers, and Writers* (Grand Rapids, MI: Baker Books, 2002), 70.

21. Ibid.

22. Ray Stedman, *From Guilt to Glory*, Volume 21 (Waco, TX: Word, 1978), 136.

23. Michael P. Green, ed., *Illustrations for Biblical Preaching*, "Prayer, Answers to" (Grand Rapids, MI: Baker Book House, 1991), 274.

24. *The Kneeling Christian* (New Kensington, PA: Whitaker House, 2013), preface.

25. Bill Hybels, *Too Busy Not to Pray* (Downers Grove, IL: InterVarsity Press, 1998), 9.

26. Compiled by Martin H. Manser, *The Westminster Collection of Christian Quotations* (Louisville: Westminster John Knox Press, 2001), 220.

Topical Index